New Common Entrance Mathematics

Workbook

Second Edition

Walter Phillips BA
Head of Mathematics
St. Lucy Secondary School, Barbados

Stanley Thornes (Publishers) Ltd

First published in 1986 by:
Stanley Thornes (Publishers) Ltd
Delta Place
27 Bath Road
CHELTENHAM
GL53 7TH
United Kingdom

Second Edition 1994

00 / 10   9   8   7

A catalogue record of this book is available from the British Library.

ISBN 0-7487-1759-5

Typeset by Tech-Set, Gateshead, Tyne & Wear
Printed and bound in China by Dah Hua Printing Press Co. Ltd.

Contents

Preface

There are 25 Papers and 2 Test Papers in this book. Each Paper consists of 50 questions and each test consists of 100 questions. Each Paper contains a variety of problems based on topics from the Textbook and they are graded with approximately the same degree of difficulty.

All of the 25 Papers should be done at school under the supervision of the teacher; pupils should be given no more than 40 minutes and 75 minutes respectively to complete each of the 25 Papers and each of the Test Papers.

Two Papers followed by corrections should be done each week and the two Test Papers should be done at a suitable time just leading up to the Common Entrance Examination.

However, this Workbook should only be used after the pupils have completed most of the new topics from the Textbook. A most convenient time to begin using the Workbook is at the beginning of the second term.

Walter Phillips
1994

Paper 1

Write the missing number in each of the following series:

1.	3,	8,	13,	...
2.	1000,	100,	10,	...
3.	2,	3,	5,	8,	...
4.	1,	4,	9,	16,	...
5.	3.04,	3.06,	3.08,	...

Write in figures:

6. Five thousand and ten. $Ans = ...$

7. Twelve thousand and one. $Ans = ...$

8. Add
$$674$$
$$69$$
$$+\ 208$$
$$\overline{}$$

10. Multiply
$$706$$
$$\times\ \ 8$$
$$\overline{}$$

9. Subtract
$$970$$
$$-\ 93$$
$$\overline{}$$

11. Divide
$$6424 \div 8$$
$$= ...$$

Use one of the signs ($<$, $=$, $>$) in each space to make each statement correct:

12. $3 + 8 ... 5 \times 2$

13. $17 - 3 \ldots 14 \times 0$

14. $3 \times 3 \ldots 2 \times 2 \times 2$

15. $36 \div 9 \ldots 25 - 21$

16. $\begin{array}{r} 483 \\ \times\ 70 \\ \hline \\ \hline \end{array}$ **17.** $\begin{array}{r} 687 \\ \times\ 43 \\ \hline \\ \hline \end{array}$ **18.** $8650 \div 25$
$= \ldots$

Write the following numbers in words:

19. 4670   *Ans* $= \ldots$

20. 14 085   *Ans* $= \ldots$

21. The difference of 2 numbers is 16. If the smaller number is 38, what is the bigger number?   *Ans* $= \ldots$

22. The product of 2 numbers is 72. If one number is 6, what is the other number?   *Ans* $= \ldots$

23. At most, how many times can 9 be taken from 135?

Ans $= \ldots$

Complete the following correctly:

24. $480 = 4 \times 100 + \ldots \times 10$

25. $196 = \ldots \times 10 + 6 \times 1$

26. $652 = 6 \times 100 + 5 \times 10 + \ldots \times 1$

27. At a certain Junior School there are three hundred pupils. If there are one hundred and sixty-five girls, how many boys are there?   *Ans* $= \ldots$

Use two signs from here $(+, -, \times, \div)$, one in each space, to make each statement correct:

28. $8 \ldots 4 = 17 \ldots 15$

29. $8 \ldots 7 = 14 \ldots 4$

30. $7 \ldots 0 = 6 \ldots 6$

31. $40 \ldots 5 = 19 \ldots 11$

32. $7 \ldots 8 = 60 \ldots 4$

33. $12 \ldots 1 = 11 \ldots 1$

34. What number when divided by 8 gives 16 remainder 6?

$$Ans = \ldots$$

35. What is the smallest number that must be added to 5621 to make a number that is divisible exactly by 12?

$$Ans = \ldots$$

36. A bus conductor had tickets numbered from 1 to 100. He sold tickets numbered from 45 to 60. How many tickets had he left? $Ans = \ldots$

37. Eighteen times 16 is equal to 12 times a number. What is the number? $Ans = \ldots$

Find the value of the following:

38. $4 + 5 \times 3 = \ldots$

39. $7 \times 6 - 4 = \ldots$

40. $72 \div 8 + 4 = \ldots$

41. $(7 + 8) \times 9 = \ldots$

42. $56 \div (4 + 3) = \ldots$

43. $(9 \times 5) + (6 \times 8) = \ldots$

44. Sally-Ann picked 65 green plums and 3 times as many red plums. How many plums did she pick in all?

$$Ans = \ldots$$

45. This year a cricketer scored 800 runs. Last year he scored 3 runs less. How many runs does he need to score next year, to total 2000 runs for the 3 years? $Ans = \ldots$

Complete the following:

46. $\dfrac{3}{5} = \dfrac{}{20}$

48. $\dfrac{6}{25} = \dfrac{18}{}$

47. $\dfrac{}{8} = \dfrac{15}{24}$

49. $\dfrac{2}{} = \dfrac{14}{21}$

50. The perimeter of a square is 48 cm. What is the area of the square? $Ans = \ldots$ cm^2

Paper **2**

1. $6745 + 693 + 2082 = \ldots$

2. $9701 - 938 = \ldots$

3. $\begin{array}{r} 7063 \\ \times \quad 8 \\ \hline \\ \hline \end{array}$

4. $8424 \div 12 = \ldots$

Write in figures:

5. Fifteen thousand and twelve. $Ans = \ldots$

6. Twenty thousand, six hundred and eight. $Ans = \ldots$

7. $\begin{array}{r} 432 \\ \times \quad 76 \\ \hline \\ \hline \end{array}$

8. $7475 \div 23 = \ldots$

What is the value of each letter in the following equations?

9. $a - 4 = 12 \quad \therefore \quad a = \ldots$

10. $x + 7 = 18 \quad \therefore \quad x = \ldots$

11. $b + b = 30 \quad \therefore \quad b = \ldots$

12. $21 - n = 5 \quad \therefore \quad n = \ldots$

13. $m \times m = 64 \quad \therefore \quad m = \ldots$

14. $\dfrac{t}{4} = 8 \quad \therefore \quad t = \ldots$

15. If an exercise book costs $0.85, find the cost of 12 similar exercise books. $Ans = \$\ldots$

16. $\frac{1}{3}$ of a number is 15. What is the number? $Ans = \ldots$

4

17. The perimeter of the figure
to the right is 41 cm.
Find the length of the
side marked t.

9 cm · 8 cm · t · 14 cm

$Ans\ =\ \ldots$ cm

18. Find the average of 16, 48, 74 and 30. $Ans\ =\ \ldots$

Write in words:

19. 40 705 $Ans\ =\ \ldots$

20. 12 006 $Ans\ =\ \ldots$

21. Nadia is 148 cm tall. Fiona is 6 cm shorter than Nadia.
What is the sum of their heights? $Ans\ =\ \ldots$ cm

22. The difference of two numbers is 78. If the larger number
is 206, what is the other number? $Ans\ =\ \ldots$

23. $\dfrac{3}{4} - \dfrac{1}{2} = \ldots$ **24.** $\dfrac{1}{3} + \dfrac{2}{5} = \ldots$

Complete:

25. $2\frac{1}{2}$ h $= \ldots$ min

26. 240 s $= \ldots$ min

27. Subtract

$$
\begin{array}{rr}
\text{h} & \text{min} \\
16 & 15 \\
-\ \ 6 & 40 \\
\hline
\end{array}
$$

Use all of the digits (3, 6, 1, 5) once only to form:

28. The largest possible number. $Ans\ =\ \ldots$

29. The smallest possible number. $Ans\ =\ \ldots$

30. If 4 similar pencils cost $1.00, find the cost of 7 of these
pencils. $Ans\ =\ \$\ldots$

Divide 60 golden apples between Ann and June so that June gets 4 more than Ann.

31. June gets . . . golden apples

32. Ann gets . . . golden apples

Use two signs from here $(+, -, \times, \div)$, one in each space, to make correct statements:

33. $4 \ldots 3 \ldots 2 = 14$

34. $5 \ldots 6 \ldots 2 = 15$

35. $8 \ldots 3 \ldots 4 = 9$

36. $42 \ldots (5 \ldots 1) = 7$

37. $(6 \ldots 3) \ldots 9 = 1$

38. $(4 \ldots 4) \ldots 4 = 0$

Complete:

39. $\dfrac{16}{25} = \ldots \%$

40. $\dfrac{26}{40} = \ldots \%$

41. $30\% = \dfrac{}{10}$

42. $85\% = \dfrac{17}{}$

43. Add

m	cm
3	47
2	69
+	76

44. Divide

$\$54.36 \div 9$

$= \$ \ldots$

The graph below shows the number of shirt jacs sold by a department store during a 6-day week.

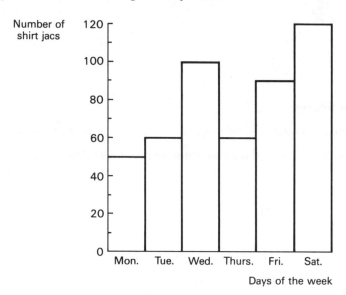

45. How many shirt jacs were sold on Monday? *Ans* = ...
On which two days were the same number of shirt jacs sold?

46. *Ans* = ...   **47.** *Ans* = ...

48. What was the greatest number of shirt jacs sold for any one day?   *Ans* = ...

49. What was the average number of shirt jacs sold per day for the week?   *Ans* = ...

50. What is the square root of 169?   *Ans* = ...

Paper **3**

Write in figures:

1. Thirty thousand and one. *Ans* = ...

2. Two hundred and ten thousand and seventy. *Ans* = ...

Complete:

3. 530 = ... tens

4. 2006 = ... tens + 6 ones

5. 423 = ... hundreds + 2 tens + 3 ones

6. Subtract

$	¢
118	30
− 78	67

7. Multiply

370
× 80
_____

8. Add

86
874
+ 278
_____

9. The area of a square is 64 cm^2. What is its perimeter?

Ans = ... cm

10. A school lesson started at 9.40 a.m. and lasted for 40 min. At what time did it end? *Ans* = ...

Write the missing number in each series:

11. 6, 12, 18, ...

12. 10, 11, 13, 16, ...

13. 1, 0.1, 0.01, 0.001, ...

14. 4, 2, 1, $\frac{1}{2}$, ...

15. 144, 121, 100, 81, ...

Divide 100 plums between Peter and Paul so that every time Peter gets 2 plums, Paul gets 3 plums.

16. When Peter gets 6 plums, how many does Paul get?

$$Ans = \ldots$$

17. When Paul get 24 plums, how many does Peter get?

$$Ans = \ldots$$

18. How many plums does Peter get out of the 100 plums?

$$Ans = \ldots$$

19. How many plums does Paul get out of the 100 plums?

$$Ans = \ldots$$

20. Sonia had $5.00 for pocket money. She spent half of it at the village shop and $1.65 at the school canteen. How much had she left? $\quad Ans = \$\ldots$

Find the value of each letter in the following equations:

21. $x + x + x = 42 \quad \therefore \quad x = \ldots$

22. $20 - m = 4 \quad \therefore \quad m = \ldots$

23. $3 \times p = 36 \quad \therefore \quad p = \ldots$

24. $(n \times n) - 3 = 22 \quad \therefore \quad n = \ldots$

25. $2a - 1 = 15 \quad \therefore \quad a = \ldots$

26. $\dfrac{40}{c} = 5 \quad \therefore \quad c = \ldots$

27. $5 - 2.64 = \ldots$

28. $18.7 + 9.34 = \ldots$

Find the value of:

29. 10% of 80. $\quad Ans = \ldots$

30. 5% of $300. $\quad Ans = \$\ldots$

31. A certain school had a roll of 240 pupils. One rainy day 80% of the pupils were absent from school. How many pupils were present? $\quad Ans = \ldots$

Here is part of a calendar for the month of March, 1985. Use this to help you answer the questions below.

March

Sun.	Mon.	Tue.	Wed.	Thurs.	Fri.	Sat.
					1	2
3	4	5	6	7	8	9
10	11	12	13	14	15	16

32. How many Tuesdays are there in March, 1985?

Ans = ...

33. What day of the week was the last day in February, 1985?

Ans = ...

34. 1st March is a Friday. What date was the Friday before?

Ans = ...

35. On what day of the week will the month of March, 1985 end?   *Ans* = ...

36. One sixth of a number is 12. What is the number?

Ans = ...

Write in words:
37. 15 076   *Ans* = ...
38. 125 312   *Ans* = ...

Use a sign from here ($<$, $=$, $>$) in each space to make each statement correct:

39. $14 - 4 \ldots 26 \div 2$
40. $8 \times 12 \ldots 40 + 22$
41. $6 \times 1 \ldots 6 \times 0$
42. $9 - 9 \ldots 9 - 0$

43. Find the average of $4.70, $2.92 and 72¢.   *Ans* = $...

Given that 24 × 32 = 768,

without doing any more working

write answers for:

$$
\begin{array}{r}
24 \times 32 \\
\hline
720 \\
48 \\
\hline
768 \\
\hline
\end{array}
$$

44. 768 ÷ 32 = . . .   **46.** 24 × 16 = . . .

45. 768 ÷ 24 = . . .   **47.** 48 × 32 = . . .

What kind of angle is each of the following angles below?

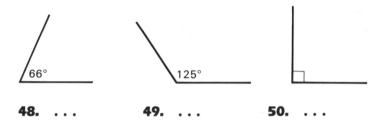

48. . . .   **49.** . . .   **50.** . . .

Paper 4

1.
$$649 \times 8$$

2. $2712 \div 8$
$= \ldots$

3. $552 \div 23$
$= \ldots$

Complete:

4. $\dfrac{3}{4} = \dfrac{15}{}$

5. $\dfrac{8}{} = \dfrac{40}{45}$

6. $\dfrac{}{4} = \dfrac{8}{32}$

7. Subtract

m	cm
16	43
− 9	60

8. Add

h	min
3	25
2	40
+ 1	28

9. Multiply

$	¢
15	70
×	9

Change the following base 2 numbers to base 10:

10. $1101_2 = \ldots$

11. $10111_2 = \ldots$

12. $3.09 + 15.6 + 0.85 = \ldots$

13. $15.3 - 6.43 = \ldots$

Complete:

14. $42 \times 36 = 42 \times 6 + 42 \times \ldots$

15. $76 \times 308 = 76 \times 300 + 76 \times \ldots$

16. $59 \times 70 = \ldots \times 7 \times 10$

The Venn diagram to the right shows the number of pupils in a certain class who like mathematics or English or both subjects.

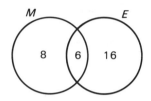

17. How many pupils like mathematics?   *Ans* = . . .

18. How many pupils like English?   *Ans* = . . .

19. How many pupils like mathematics only?   *Ans* = . . .

20. How many pupils like both subjects?   *Ans* = . . .

21. It takes Carlo 15 min to walk to school. At what time must he leave home to get to school at 8.40 a.m.?

         Ans = . . .

Divide 120 marbles between John and Peter so that John gets twice as much as Peter.

22. John gets . . . marbles

23. Peter gets . . . marbles

In the number 427.683, the value of the 3 is 3 thousandths.

24. The value of the 2 is 2 . . .

25. The value of the 4 is 4 . . .

26. The value of the 6 is 6 . . .

27. The value of the 7 is 7 . . .

28. The value of the 8 is 8 . . .

29. A farmer had 400 birds. He killed 60% of them. How many birds remained alive?   *Ans* = . . .

Use names from the list (rectangle, circle, cylinder, cone, cuboid, triangle, sphere) to describe the figures below:

30.
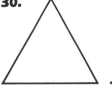
...

33.
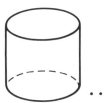
...

31.
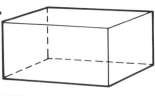
...

34.
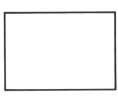
...

32.
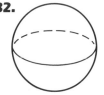
...

35. $\dfrac{2}{3} - \dfrac{3}{5} =$ ...

37. $\dfrac{2}{5} \times \dfrac{5}{8} =$ ...

36. $\dfrac{1}{2} + \dfrac{4}{5} =$ ...

38. What is $\frac{1}{4}$ of 136? *Ans* = ...

39. Four exercise books cost the same as 3 pens. If a pen costs $1.20, what is the cost of an exercise book? *Ans* = $...

Write the following decimals as fractions in their lowest terms:

e.g. $0.3 = \dfrac{3}{10}$, $0.08 = \dfrac{8}{100} = \dfrac{2}{25}$

40. $0.7 =$ ...

42. $0.16 =$ ...

41. $0.2 =$ ...

43. $0.60 =$ ...

44. The average of 5 numbers is 42. What is the sum of these 5 numbers? *Ans* = ...

Calculate the value of the angles marked x:

45.

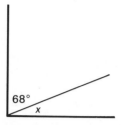

Angle x = ...

46.

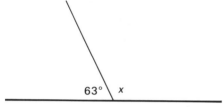

Angle x = ...

Use two signs from here (+, −, ×, ÷), one in each space, to make each statement correct:

47. 4 . . . 3 . . . 8 = 4

48. (11 . . . 5) . . . 1 = 6

49. 5 . . . 3 . . . 8 = 0

50. (7 . . . 4) . . . 2 = 6

Paper 5

1. $872 \div 8$

$= \ldots$

2. $\begin{array}{r} 674 \\ \times \quad 9 \\ \hline \\ \hline \end{array}$

3. $\begin{array}{r} 480 \\ \times \quad 63 \\ \hline \\ \hline \end{array}$

4. $7025 \div 25$

$= \ldots$

5. Write in figures: eighty thousand, one hundred and ten.

$Ans = \ldots$

6. What is the difference between 1070 and 684?

$Ans = \ldots$

7. $\frac{3}{4}$ of the money in my purse is \$75.00. How much money do I have in my purse? $Ans = \$ \ldots$

8. $1\frac{1}{2} + 1\frac{1}{3}$

$= \ldots$

10. $\frac{8}{15} \times \frac{3}{4}$

$= \ldots$

9. $1\frac{1}{2} - \frac{7}{8}$

$= \ldots$

11. $\frac{3}{5} \div \frac{2}{3}$

$= \ldots$

12. What is $\frac{1}{2}$ of 1.70 m? $Ans = \ldots$ m

13. $\frac{1}{8}$ of a number is 16. What is the number? $Ans = \ldots$

14. In a certain private car park there were 240 cars. If 15% of them were Datsuns, how many cars were not Datsuns?

$Ans = \ldots$

15. What is the square root of 256? $Ans = \ldots$

16. $15 - 2.64 = \ldots$

17. $18.7 + 9.34 + 12 = \ldots$

18. $6.74 \times 0.6 = \ldots$

19. $0.376 \div 8 = \ldots$

20. Subtract

    h   min

    13   15

  − 3   43

  ──────

21. Divide

    min s

  6⟌19 06

22. The average of 5 numbers is 67. Four of these numbers are 23, 16, 89 and 58. Find the 5th number. *Ans* $= \ldots$

23. What is the smallest number that must be subtracted from 1500 to make a number that is divisible exactly by 8? *Ans* $= \ldots$

Study the diagram below and then answer the questions that follow.

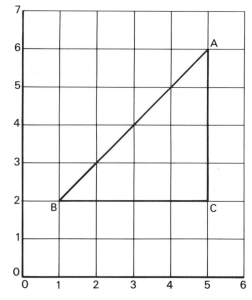

24. What is the area of the triangle ABC? *Ans* $= \ldots$ cm^2

25. The coordinates of A $= (\ldots)$

26. The coordinates of B $= (\ldots)$

27. The coordinates of C $= (\ldots)$

Complete:

28. 3 cm = ... mm   **30.** 60 mm = ... cm

29. 4.5 cm = ... mm   **31.** 225 cm = ... m

From this set of numbers {1, 2, 3, 4, 5, 6, 7, 8, 9, 10}, pick out:

32. The smallest prime number.   *Ans* = ...

33. The largest prime number.   *Ans* = ...

34. Flying fish are sold at 5 for $1.00. How much would 12 flying fish cost?   *Ans* = $...

If $a = 4$ and $b = 3$, find the value of:

35. $a + 2b$ = ...   **38.** $3ab - 2b^2$ = ...

36. $a^2 + b^2$ = ...   **39.** $2a + b$ = ...

37. $ab - 5$ = ...

40. A TV programme began at 18:45 hours and lasted for 35 min.

At what time did it end?   *Ans* = ...

41. What is 10% of $200.00?   *Ans* = $...

Find the value of each letter in the following equations:

42. $a + 7 = 11$ $\therefore$ a = ...

43. $m - 6 = 12$ $\therefore$ m = ...

44. $21 - n = 5$ $\therefore$ n = ...

45. $x \times 8 = 40$ $\therefore$ x = ...

46. $y \times y + 1 = 26$ $\therefore$ y = ...

Divide $60.00 between Mary and June so that Mary gets $4.00 more than June:

47. June gets $...

48. Mary gets $...

Complete:

49. 2.5 kg = ... g

50. 3000 g = ... kg

Paper 6

1. Subtract

$$\begin{array}{r} \$ \quad ¢ \\ 120 \quad 36 \\ -\ 89 \quad 70 \\ \hline \\ \hline \end{array}$$

2. Multiply

$$\begin{array}{r} \$ \quad ¢ \\ 13 \quad 45 \\ \times \qquad 9 \\ \hline \\ \hline \end{array}$$

3. Subtract

$$\begin{array}{r} 2065 \\ -\ 1074 \\ \hline \\ \hline \end{array}$$

4. $3160 \div 20$

$= \ldots$

5. $1598 \div 34$

$= \ldots$

6. $\begin{array}{r} 456 \\ \times\ 804 \\ \hline \\ \hline \end{array}$

7. $1\frac{1}{3} + 1\frac{3}{4}$

$= \ldots$

8. $1\frac{5}{8} - \frac{2}{3}$

$= \ldots$

9. $\frac{3}{5} \times 1\frac{1}{6}$

$= \ldots$

10. $4 \div 1\frac{1}{3}$

$= \ldots$

11. What is $\frac{1}{5}$ of 2.5 kg?   *Ans* $= \ldots$ g

12. $5 + 3.86 + 25.9 = \ldots$

13. $18.3 - 7.24 = \ldots$

14. $8.07 \times 0.07 = \ldots$

15. $3.85 \div 0.5 = \ldots$

16. What is 90% of $200?   *Ans* $= \$ \ldots$

17. Aunt May has $5.00 in her purse, made up of 5¢ and 10¢ pieces only. If she has twenty-eight 5¢ pieces, how many 10¢ pieces does she have?   *Ans* $= \ldots$

In a netball match between Class 3 and Class 4, 48 goals were scored. Class 4 scored 3 times as many goals as Class 3.

18. Class 3 scored . . . goals

19. Class 4 scored . . . goals

20. If a litre of gasoline costs $1.15, how much would 7 L cost?

$Ans = \$. . .$

21. List all the factors of 15. $Ans = . . .$

22. A cyclist travelled 400 m in 25 s. What was his average speed in metres per second? (i.e. how far did he travel in 1 s?) $Ans = . . .$ m per second

Complete:

23. $3\frac{1}{2}$ min $= . . .$ s

24. 420 s $= . . .$ min

25. 5 weeks $= . . .$ days

26. 217 days $= . . .$ weeks

If $A = \{1, 2, 3, 4, 5, 6, 7\}$ and $B = \{2, 4, 6, 8\}$:

27. What is $A \cup B$? $Ans = . . .$

28. What is $A \cap B$? $Ans = . . .$

The diagram to the right shows a square ABCD. Each side of the square is 12 cm.

29. What is the area of square ABCD? $Ans = . . .$ cm^2

30. What is the area of the shaded triangle?

$Ans = . . .$ cm^2

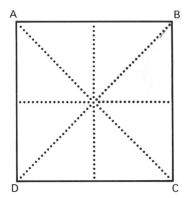

Find the value of:

31. $12 + 6 \times 7 = . . .$ **32.** $5 + 3 \times 4 + 8 = . . .$

33. $(16 - 4) \times (15 + 3) = . . .$

34. $19 - 5 \times 2 + 8 = . . .$

Use a name from here (acute, obtuse, right, straight, reflex) to describe each angle below:

35.

. . . angle

37.

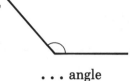

. . . angle

36.

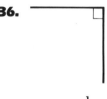

. . . angle

What is the value of each letter in the following equations?

38. $a - 7 = 12$ $\therefore$ $a = $ . . .

39. $24 - c = 6$ $\therefore$ $c = $ . . .

40. $m \times m - 1 = 80$ $\therefore$ $m = $ . . .

41. $3 \times y + 5 = 23$ $\therefore$ $y = $ . . .

A shopkeeper bought a case of 24 soft drinks for $10.00. She sold them at 60¢ each.

42. How much profit did she make? *Ans* = $. . .

43. What was her percentage profit? *Ans* = . . .%

Draw in all the lines of symmetry in the following figures:

44.

Rectangle

46.

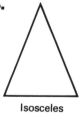

Isosceles
triangle

45.

Semicircle

Uncle Joe divided 60 cherries between Ryan and his brother Robert in the ratio 2 : 3.

47. Ryan received . . . cherries

48. Robert received . . . cherries

49. What is the square root of 225? *Ans* = . . .

In the diagram the angles marked with the same letter are equal.

50. Angle d = . . . degrees

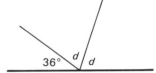

Paper 7

$3192 \div 42 = 76$

Use the above result to write answers for the following:

1. $3192 \div 76 = \ldots$ **3.** $3192 \div 84 = \ldots$

2. $42 \times 76 = \ldots$ **4.** $3192 \div 21 = \ldots$

Write in figures:

5. Thirty thousand and seven.   *Ans* $= \ldots$

6. Two hundred and ten thousand and twenty.

Ans $= \ldots$

7. $\$78.72 + \$613.05 + \$6.98 = \$\ldots$

8.
$$\begin{array}{r} 489 \\ \times\ \ 7 \\ \hline \\ \hline \end{array}$$

10. $1404 \div 27$
$= \ldots$

12. Subtract

cm	mm
27	3
− 17	8

9.
$$\begin{array}{r} 407 \\ \times\ 80 \\ \hline \\ \hline \end{array}$$

11. Multiply

h	min
15	11
×	6

13. $6.4 - 0.64$
$= \ldots$

14. $0.917 \times 0.06 = \ldots$

15. $4.5 \div 0.5 = \ldots$

16. $6.9 + 14.76 + 0.29 = \ldots$

17. $\frac{3}{10} + \frac{1}{2}$ **18.** $4\frac{1}{2} - \frac{7}{8}$ **19.** $2\frac{1}{2} \times 1\frac{3}{5}$ **20.** $\frac{3}{4} \div 1\frac{1}{2}$
$= \ldots$ $= \ldots$ $= \ldots$ $= \ldots$

21. What is the remainder when 400 is divided by 12?

$$Ans = \ldots$$

Delcia had 140 hibiscus plants. She sold $\frac{3}{4}$ of them at the Holetown Festival.

22. How many did she sell? $\qquad$ $Ans = \ldots$

23. How many remained unsold? $\qquad$ $Ans = \ldots$

Use all of the digits from here (3, 2, 6, 7), once only, to form:

24. The smallest possible number. $\qquad$ $Ans = \ldots$

25. The largest possible number. $\qquad$ $Ans = \ldots$

26. The smallest possible even number. $\qquad$ $Ans = \ldots$

27. The largest possible even number. $\qquad$ $Ans = \ldots$

28. The smallest possible odd number. $\qquad$ $Ans = \ldots$

29. In the diagram, find the area of the shaded border.

$Ans = \ldots$ cm^2

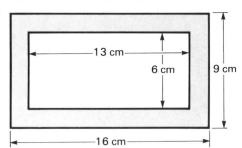

In the diagram, angle $a = 90°$. PQ is a straight line and angles marked with the same letter are equal.

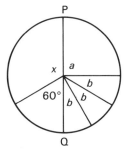

30. Angle $b = \ldots$ degrees

31. Angle $x = \ldots$ degrees

Use a sign from here ($<$, $=$, $>$) in each space to make each statement correct:

32. $6 \times 6 \ldots 6 + 6$ $\qquad$ **34.** $8 \times 0 \ldots 7 + 1$

33. $18 \div 9 \ldots 1 \times 1$ $\qquad$ **35.** $72 \div 18 \ldots 2^2$

In the diagram below, what are:

36. The coordinates of D? (. . .)

37. The coordinates of E? (. . .)

38. The coordinates of F? (. . .)

39. The coordinates of G? (. . .)

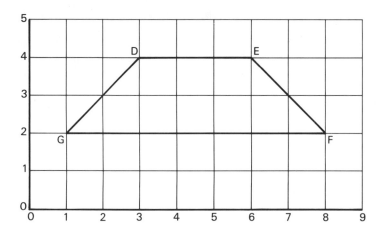

40. Is the figure a parallelogram, rhombus, trapezium or rectangle? *Ans* = . . .

41. What is the area of this figure? *Ans* = . . . cm²

42. How much Barbados currency is equivalent to US $40.00 if US $1.00 = BB $1.98? *Ans* = BB $. . .

43. A pair of shoes which usually costs $36.00 was reduced by 10%. How much must a customer pay for them?

Ans = $. . .

44. A taxi driver buys 20 L of gasoline every day. If 1 L of gasoline costs $1.15, how much had he spent on gasoline at the end of a five-day week? *Ans* = $. . .

45. If three similar reading books cost $24.00, how much would eight of them cost at the same price? *Ans* = $. . .

Pedro was born on 24th June, 1973.

46. How old was he on 24th December, 1984?

Ans = . . . years . . . months

47. On what date was Pedro 9 years old?   *Ans* = ...

48. What is the cost of 3.6 kg of cabbage at $2.50 per kg?

$$Ans = \$...$$

Change the following base 5 numbers to base 10:

49. 423_5 = ...   **50.** 210_5 = ...

Paper 8

Complete:

1. $390 = \dots$ ones

2. $817 = \dots \times 10 + 7 \times 1$

3. $2765 = \dots \times 100 + 65 \times 1$

4. $307 \times 200 = \dots$

5. $696 \div 29 = \dots$

6. $1876 - 909 = \dots$

7. $\frac{3}{4} + \frac{2}{5} = \dots$

8. $3\frac{1}{2} - 2\frac{3}{5} = \dots$

9. $\frac{3}{8} \times 1\frac{1}{3} = \dots$

10. $2\frac{1}{2} \div 1\frac{2}{3} = \dots$

11. $14.0 - 6.43 = \dots$

12. $42 \div 0.6 = \dots$

Look at the triangle to the right.

13. What is its perimeter?

$$Ans = \dots \text{cm}$$

14. What is its area?

$$Ans = \dots \text{cm}^2$$

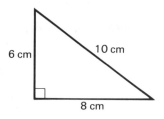

6 cm   10 cm

8 cm

15. Our school radio programme begins at 09:40 hours and lasts for 45 min. At what time does it finish? $Ans = \dots$

16. How many days are there in February 1990? $Ans = \dots$

17. How many lengths of string each 0.75 m long can be cut from a length of string measuring 6 m? $Ans = \dots$

From this set of numbers $\{1, 2, 3, 4, 5, 6, 7, 8, 9\}$ pick out:

18. All the factors of 4. $Ans = \dots$

19. All the multiples of 2. $Ans = \dots$

27

20. Sam, the village farmer, had 80 head of cattle. He sold half of them and killed 25% of what remained. How many head of cattle had he left?   *Ans* = ...

Calculate the value of the angles marked with letters. Angles marked with the same letter are equal.

21.

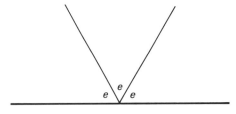

Angles *e* = ... degrees

22.

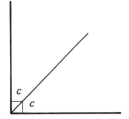

Angles *c* = ... degrees

23.

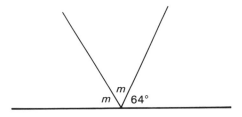

Angles *m* = ... degrees

24. A pencil costs 25¢ and a ruler costs 30¢. I bought 7 pencils and 7 rulers. How much change should I receive if I give the cashier $5.00?   *Ans* = $...

Solve the following equations:

25. $m - 17 = 7$ ∴ m = ...

26. $26 = 3 \times p + 2$ ∴ p = ...

27. $(n + n) - 4 = 16$ $\therefore$ $n = \ldots$

28. $y \times y = 144$ $\therefore$ $y = \ldots$

29. $20 - x = 5$ $\therefore$ $x = \ldots$

30. $\dfrac{a}{4} = 16$ $\therefore$ $a = \ldots$

An aircraft travels at 400 km per hour.

31. How far does it travel in 45 min?   *Ans* $= \ldots$ km

32. How long does it take to travel 100 km at the same rate?

Ans $= \ldots$ min

Use two signs from here $(+, -, \times, \div)$, one in each space, to make each statement correct:

33. $48 \ldots 6 = 1 \ldots 8$

34. $9 \ldots 0 = 15 \ldots 15$

35. $72 \ldots 18 = 16 \ldots 4$

36. $5 \ldots 13 = 9 \ldots 2$

37. Our Mini Austin travels 12 km on 1 L of gasoline. How many litres would it use in travelling 156 km?

Ans $= \ldots$ L

In the diagram to the right

$C = \{$Pupils who play cricket$\}$

$F = \{$Pupils who play football$\}$

$T = \{$Pupils who play tennis$\}$

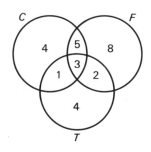

38. How many pupils play cricket?   *Ans* $= \ldots$

39. How many pupils play football?   *Ans* $= \ldots$

40. How many pupils play tennis?   *Ans* $= \ldots$

41. How many pupils play tennis only?   *Ans* $= \ldots$

42. How many pupils play all three games?   *Ans* $= \ldots$

43. How many pupils play both football and tennis?

Ans $= \ldots$

Use a name from here (triangle, rectangle, cone, sphere, circle, cuboid, cylinder) to describe each of the objects below:

44. A football is a . . .

45. A sheet from your workbook is a . . .

46. A shoe box is a . . .

47. An Ovaltine tin is a . . .

48. The rim of a tea cup is a . . .

49. A dollar note is a . . .

50. If 12 exercise books cost $7.80, how much would 5 of these exercise books cost?   *Ans* = $ . . .

Paper **9**

Write the missing number in each series:

1.	12,	18,	. . . ,	30,	36

2.	6,	7,	9,	12,	. . .

3.	1.00,	1.50,	2.00,	. . .

4.	16,	25,	36,	49,	. . .

5.	1,	8,	27,	64,	. . .

Write in figures:

6. Seventy thousand three hundred and ten.   *Ans* = . . .

7. Thirty thousand and six.   *Ans* = . . .

8. Three hundred and five dollars and five cents.

   Ans = $. . .

9. Add together: Five hundred and twenty, six thousand and one, and nineteen.   *Ans* = . . .

10. From two thousand and twenty take nine hundred and eight.   *Ans* = . . .

11. $1505 \div 8$

   = . . .

13. $3392 \div 32$

   = . . .

12.   609

   $\times$ 12

   ‾‾‾‾

Complete:

14. $\dfrac{5}{6} = \dfrac{20}{\quad}$ **15.** $\dfrac{1}{\quad} = \dfrac{4}{24}$ **16.** $\dfrac{2}{3} = \dfrac{3 \times}{18}$

17. $1\frac{1}{2} + 2\frac{2}{3} =$ ...   **19.** $\frac{8}{15} \times 1\frac{3}{4} =$ ...

18. $2\frac{3}{4} - 1\frac{2}{3} =$ ...

In the number 7306.125, 0 = 0 tens. Find the value of:

20. 1 = 1 ...   **23.** 5 = 5 ...

21. 2 = 2 ...   **24.** 6 = 6 ...

22. 3 = 3 ...   **25.** 7 = 7 ...

26. What is 0.5 of 700 g?   *Ans* = ... g

27. 12 + 8.2 + 16.38 = ...

28. 19.16 − 8.4 = ...

29. 0.637 × 0.06 = ...

30. 4.75 ÷ 0.5 = ...

31. A piece of string 7.60 m long is divided into 8 equal pieces. What is the length of each piece?

                                            Ans = ... cm

32. What is the square root of 400?   *Ans* = ...

Mother had \$60.00 to divide among her three children. She gave $\frac{1}{3}$ of it to Sharon, $\frac{1}{4}$ of it to Jennifer and the rest to Jerry.

33. Sharon received \$ ...

34. Jennifer received \$ ...

35. Jerry received \$ ...

36. Miss Alleyne sells sugar cakes at 15¢ each. One day she collected \$5.25 for sugar cakes. How many sugar cakes did she sell?   *Ans* = ...

A dealer bought an article for \$400.00 and sold it for \$520.

37. What was his profit?   *Ans* = \$ ...

38. What was his percentage profit?   *Ans* = ... %

Complete, by looking at the diagram below:

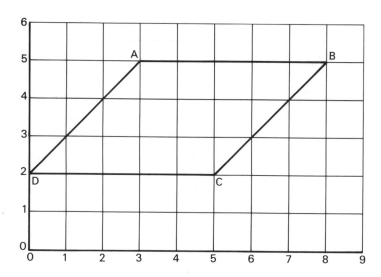

39. The coordinates of A = (...)

40. The coordinates of B = (...)

41. The coordinates of C = (...)

42. The coordinates of D = (...)

43. The area of ABCD = ... cm²

44. Use a name from the list to describe figure ABCD (parallelogram, rhombus, rectangle, trapezium).

Ans = ...

Divide 240 marbles between Dwayne and Calvin so that Calvin gets thrice (three times) as many as Dwayne.

45. Dwayne gets ... marbles

46. Calvin gets ... marbles

The following lines are drawn to a scale of 1 cm = 5 m. Measure them and write down their measurements in metres.

47. ─────────────────────

Ans = ... m

48. ─────────────────

Ans = ... m

49. ⎯⎯⎯⎯⎯⎯⎯⎯⎯⎯⎯⎯⎯⎯⎯⎯⎯⎯⎯⎯

Ans = ... m

50. ⎯⎯⎯⎯⎯⎯⎯⎯⎯⎯⎯⎯⎯⎯⎯⎯⎯⎯⎯⎯⎯

Ans = ...m

Paper **10**

1. $\begin{array}{rr} \$ & \cent \\ 17 & 09 \\ \times & 12 \end{array}$ _____

2. $\$64.32 \div 8$ = \$. . .

3. $6150 \div 50$ = . . .

4. $\begin{array}{r} 840 \\ \times \ 70 \\ \hline \end{array}$

5. What number added to 63 gives 91?   _Ans_ = . . .

Complete:

6. $\dfrac{2}{-} = \dfrac{16}{40}$ **7.** $\dfrac{3}{5} = \dfrac{15}{-}$ **8.** $\dfrac{3}{8} = \dfrac{9 \times}{24}$

9. $1\frac{3}{4} + 2\frac{1}{2} =$ . . .   **12.** $12 \div 2\frac{2}{3} =$ . . .

10. $\frac{2}{3} - \frac{1}{4} =$ . . .   **13.** $0.04 \times 0.04 =$ . . .

11. $3\frac{1}{5} \times 1\frac{1}{4} =$ . . .   **14.** $1.648 \div 0.08 =$ . . .

Complete:

15. $60\% = \dfrac{3}{-}$ **16.** $15\% = \dfrac{}{20}$

17. In our village there are 40 houses. 90% of them have electricity. How many houses do not have electricity?

Ans = . . .

Write a decimal point in each of the following numbers so that the 5 has the value of 5 tenths:

18. 4576   _Ans_ = . . .   **20.** 5079   _Ans_ = . . .

19. 1350   _Ans_ = . . .   **21.** 3915   _Ans_ = . . .

Complete:

22. 4 kg = . . . g   **24.** 0.8 kg = . . . g

23. 1.5 kg = . . . g   **25.** 2600 g = . . . kg

26. Dion rides to school in 35 min. At what time must he leave home to arrive at school at 08:15 hours?   *Ans* = . . .

27. Today is 27th July. Michael's birthday is exactly two weeks away. What date is Michael's birthday?

Ans = . . .

28. The average of 3 numbers is 45 and the average of 2 other numbers is 60. What is the average of the 5 numbers?

Ans = . . .

The figure to the right is made up of a square of length 14 cm and a semicircle. The area of the figure is 273 cm^2.

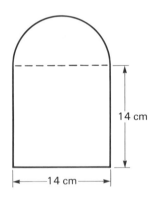

14 cm

14 cm

29. What is the area of the semicircle? *Ans* = . . . cm^2

Use two signs from here (+, −, ×, ÷), one in each space, to make each statement true:

30. 7 . . . 1 = 3 . . . 2

31. 12 . . . 3 = 8 . . . 4

32. 6 . . . 0 = 6 . . . 1

33. 5 . . . 5 = 16 . . . 9

If P = {1, 3, 5, 7, 9} and Q = {2, 4, 6, 8}:

34. $P \cup Q$ = . . .

35. $P \cap Q$ = . . .

36. A bus travels at 60 km per hour. How far will it travel in $1\frac{1}{2}$ h?   *Ans* = ... km

37. How long will it take to travel 45 km?   *Ans* = ... min

38. What is the square root of 144?   *Ans* = ...

If $p = 2$, $q = 3$, and $r = 0$, find the value of:

39. $pq + qr = $ ...   **42.** $5p - 2q = $ ...

40. $p \times q \times r = $ ...   **43.** $3pq + 6r = $ ...

41. $p^3 + q^2 = $ ...   **44.** $4p^2 + q^3 = $ ...

Convert the following base 8 numbers to base 10:

45. $127_8 = $ ...   **46.** $3065_8 = $ ...

In the figures below draw in all the lines of symmetry:

47.
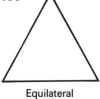
Equilateral
triangle

49.

Rhombus

48.

Square

50. The length of a rectangular piece of paper is 30 cm. If the length is twice the width, what is the width of the paper?   *Ans* = ... cm

Paper **11**

1. Take 467 from 2305. *Ans* = ...

Write in figures:

2. Twenty thousand and two. *Ans* = ...

3. Three hundred and two thousand and six. *Ans* = ...

4. 8640 ÷ 30

= ...

7. 519
× 648
_____

5.

m	cm
13	17

×   8
_____

8. 5773 ÷ 23

= ...

6. $372.45 ÷ 5

= ...

9. Subtract

min	s
26	45
− 8	30

_____

10. What is $\frac{3}{4}$ of 2 kg? *Ans* = ...g

11. What is 40% of $600? *Ans* = $...

12. My father planted 120 banana trees. The wind blew down 20% of them. How many trees were blown down?

Ans = ...

13. $1\frac{3}{8} - \frac{2}{5} = $ ...

14. $2\frac{1}{4} - 1\frac{4}{5} = $ ...

Complete:

15. $2\,\text{kg} = \ldots\text{g}$ **17.** $1825\,\text{g} = \ldots\text{kg}$

16. $3.50\,\text{kg} = \ldots\text{g}$

In the number 1490.763 the digit 9 gives the number of tens.
Which digit gives the number of:

18. thousandths? ...   **21.** ones? ...

19. tenths? ...   **22.** hundredths? ...

20. hundreds? ...   **23.** thousands? ...

24. If 3 pairs of similar jeans cost $48.00, what will 7 pairs of these jeans cost?   *Ans* $= \$\ldots$

25. $2 \times 2 \times 3 \times 3 \times 3 \times 3 = 324$, $\therefore$ the square root of $324 = \ldots$

26. Milk is sold at $1.90 per litre. How many litres of milk can $9.50 buy?   *Ans* $= \ldots\text{L}$

30 expressed as a product of prime factors $= 2 \times 3 \times 5$.
Express the following numbers as products of prime factors.

27. $28 = \ldots$ **29.** $65 = \ldots$

28. $40 = \ldots$ **30.** $105 = \ldots$

The diagram below shows the plan of the floor of a room where
1 cm on the plan represents 2 m.

31. The length of the room $= \ldots\text{m}$

32. The width of the room $= \ldots\text{m}$

33. The area of the room $= \ldots\text{m}^2$

Complete the table below:

	Distance	Speed	Time
34.	. . . km	60 km per hour	$2\frac{1}{2}$ h
35.	180 km	45 km per hour	. . .
36.	360 m	. . .	10 s

Look at the diagram below and then answer the questions that follow.

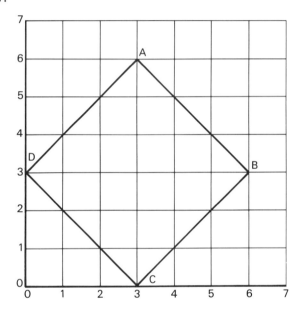

37. The coordinates of A = (. . .)

38. The coordinates of B = (. . .)

39. The coordinates of C = (. . .)

40. The coordinates of D = (. . .)

41. The figure is called a . . .

42. The area of figure ABCD = . . . cm^2

Find the value of:

43. $16 - 3 \times 5 = \ldots$

44. $(7 + 5) \times 8 = \ldots$

45. $10 + (3 \times 4) + 6 = \ldots$

46. $7 \times (3 + 6) - 15 = \ldots$

47. $8 + 6 \div 2 + 4 = \ldots$

48. $5 \times 7 + 3 \times 5 = \ldots$

Divide $5.00 between Jane and Michael so that Michael gets 40¢ more than Jane.

49. Jane gets $ . . .

50. Michael gets $ . . .

Paper **12**

1. From 1076 take 868. $Ans = \ldots$

2. $4864 \div 8$

$\quad = \ldots$

3.
$$\begin{array}{r} 706 \\ \times \quad 7 \\ \hline \\ \hline \end{array}$$

4.
$$\begin{array}{r} 461 \\ \times 293 \\ \hline \\ \hline \end{array}$$

5. How many times can I take 19 from 437? $Ans = \ldots$

6. Subtract

$	¢
240	30
− 96	73

7. Add

cm	mm
3	8
2	7
+	5

8. Multiply

h	min
8	16
×	9

Complete:

9. 98 days $= \ldots$ weeks

10. 480 s $= \ldots$ min

11. $4\frac{1}{2}$ h $= \ldots$ min

12. 34 mm $= \ldots$ cm

13. 800 cm $= \ldots$ m

14. 1.5 km $= \ldots$ m

15. June has 45 apples. Suzie has twice as many as June. How many apples do they have altogether? $Ans = \ldots$

16. In a certain school $\frac{3}{5}$ of the pupils are girls. If there are 150 boys, how many girls are there? $Ans = \ldots$

17. Sally is 1.50 m tall. Jackie is 6 cm shorter. How tall is Jackie? *Ans* = ... m

18. John runs to school at an average speed of 6 km per hour. If he runs the distance in 20 min, how far from the school does he live? *Ans* = ... km

In the number 485.76, which digit gives the number of:

19. tens ...

20. hundredths ...

21. ones ...

Change the following into decimals:

22. $\dfrac{3}{100} = \ldots$

23. $\dfrac{9}{10} = \ldots$

24. $\dfrac{16}{1000} = \ldots$

25. $7\dfrac{1}{1000} = \ldots$

26. $\dfrac{3}{4} = \ldots$

27. $\dfrac{7}{20} = \ldots$

Calculate the angles marked with letters. Angles marked with the same letter are equal.

28.

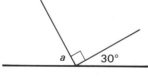

Angle a = ... degrees

29.

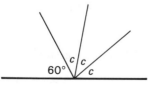

Angle c = ... degrees

30.

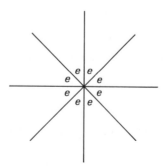

Angle e = ... degrees

31. $\dfrac{2}{5} = \dfrac{}{25}$

32. $\dfrac{2}{-} = \dfrac{16}{24}$

33. $2\frac{1}{2} - 1\frac{5}{6} = \ldots$

34. $1\frac{2}{3} \times 15 = \ldots$

35. $\dfrac{1}{2} \div \dfrac{1}{8} = \ldots$

36. 12 similar decoration blocks cost \$9.00. What is the price of 8 of these blocks?   *Ans* = \$...

What is the value of each letter in the following equations?

37. $a + 9 = 21$ $\therefore$ $a = \ldots$

38. $t - 5 = 15$ $\therefore$ $t = \ldots$

39. $m - 6 = 18$ $\therefore$ $m = \ldots$

40. $(y + y) - 3 = 31$ $\therefore$ $y = \ldots$

41. The sum of 5 consecutive even numbers is 180. What are the numbers?   *Ans* = ...

What shapes best describe the objects below?

42. A bicycle wheel is a . . .

43. A cigarette is a . . .

44. A marble is a . . .

45. Your textbook is a . . .

46. A drinking straw is a . . .

In the diagram to the right,

M = {Pupils who like Milo}

and O = {Pupils who like Ovaltine}

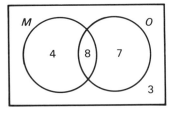

47. How many pupils like Milo?   *Ans* = ...

48. How many pupils like both Milo and Ovaltine?

        Ans = ...

49. How many pupils like neither Milo nor Ovaltine?

        Ans = ...

50. How many pupils do not like Milo?   *Ans* = ...

Paper **13**

Write the missing number in each of the following series:

1.	10,	11,	13,	16,	. . .

2.	$\frac{1}{2}$,	$\frac{1}{4}$,	$\frac{1}{8}$,	$\frac{1}{16}$,	. . .

3.	27,	9,	3,	1,	. . .

4.	1,	3,	7,	13,	. . .

5.	3.7,	3.8,	3.9,	. . .

Write in figures:

6. Thirteen thousand, three hundred and five. *Ans* = . . .

7. Eight hundred and two thousand and ten. *Ans* = . . .

Change the following base 10 numbers to base 2:

8. 15 = . . .   **9.** 20 = . . .   **10.** 9 = . . .

11. Find the sum of 76, 887 and 1076.   *Ans* = . . .

12. 8119 ÷ 9

= . . .

13.   748

× 70

‾‾‾‾‾

14. 7009 ÷ 43

= . . .

15. $2\frac{1}{3} - 1\frac{3}{4}$ = . . .

16. $4\frac{1}{2} \times \frac{2}{3}$ = . . .

17. $\frac{2}{3} \div 6$ = . . .

18. A farmer sold $\frac{1}{3}$ of his chickens to a minimart and $\frac{1}{4}$ to the village shop. What fraction of his chickens remained unsold?   *Ans* = ...

19. $8.7 + 16.84 + 0.37 = $ ...

20. $14.0 - 6.72 = $ ...

21. $6.75 \times 0.9 = $ ...

22. $4.76 \div 0.5 = $ ...

23. What is 125% of $500.00?   *Ans* = ...

24. A shopkeeper had 200 buns. She sold 25% of them at 30¢ each and the rest at 20¢ each. How much money did she get for the 200 buns?   *Ans* = ...

Calculate the values of the angles marked with letters. Angles marked with the same letter are equal.

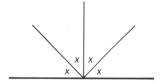 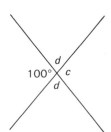

25. Angle x = ... degrees

26. Angle p = ... degrees

27. Angle $2p$ = ... degrees

28. Angle c = ... degrees

29. Angle d = ... degrees

Find the value of the following:

30. $2^2 \times 2^3 = $ ...

31. $4^2 \times 3^2 = $ ...

32. $3^3 + 3^2 = $ ...

33. $2 \times 2 \times 3 \times 3 \times 3 \times 4 = $ ...

Five similar pens cost $4.00:

34. How much would 8 of these pens cost? *Ans = $...*

35. How many of these pens can be bought for $20.00?

Ans = ...

Draw in all the lines of symmetry in the following figures:

36.  **38.**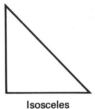

Isosceles
right-angled
triangle

37.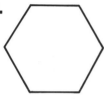

Hexagon

A teacher shares 60 crayons among Sharon, Kevin and Deon so that when Sharon receives 1 crayon, Kevin receives 2 crayons and Deon receives 3 crayons.

39. When Kevin receives 10 crayons, how many does Deon receive? *Ans = ...*

40. When Deon receives 12 crayons, how many does Sharon receive? *Ans = ...*

Out of the 60 crayons:

41. Sharon receives ... of them

42. Kevin receives ... of them

43. Deon receives ... of them

44. Without doing any calculation, what is the average of these numbers: 46, 47, 48, 49, 50? *Ans = ...*

Look at the diagram below and then answer the questions that follow:

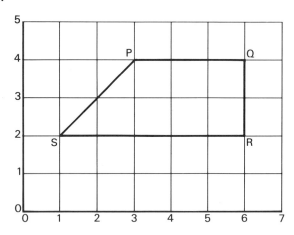

45. The coordinates of P = (. . .)

46. The coordinates of Q = (. . .)

47. The coordinates of R = (. . .)

48. The coordinates of S = (. . .)

49. What is the area of figure PQRS?   *Ans* = . . . cm^2

50. Use a name from the list to describe PQRS (rhombus, parallelogram, trapezium, rectangle).   *Ans* = . . .

Paper **14**

1. $68 \times 74 = 68 \times 4 + 68 \times \ldots$

2. $83 \times 40 + 83 \times 7 = 83 \times \ldots$

3. $2087 = \ldots \times 100 + 87 \times 1$

4. $3145 = 2 \times 1000 + \ldots \times 100 + 45 \times 1$

Use two signs from here $(+, -, \times, \div)$, one in each space, to make each statement correct:

5. $(5 \ldots 2) \ldots 4 = 12$

6. $6 \ldots 3 \ldots 2 = 4$

7. $2 \ldots 3 \ldots 2 = 8$

8. $7 \ldots 4 \ldots 3 = 0$

9. $12 \ldots 2 \ldots 3 = 18$

10. $(8 \ldots 8) \ldots 5 = 0$

11. $\begin{array}{r} 305 \\ \times\, 276 \\ \hline \\ \hline \end{array}$

12. $7956 \div 26$

   $= \ldots$

13. $\$57.40 \div 10$

   $= \ldots$

14. $1\frac{1}{2} + \frac{3}{5} = \ldots$

15. $1\frac{1}{3} - \frac{3}{8} = \ldots$

16. $\frac{4}{5} \times \frac{2}{3} = \ldots$

17. $2\frac{1}{2} \div 1\frac{1}{4} = \ldots$

18. What is $\frac{1}{12}$ of 360?   *Ans* $= \ldots$

19. $\frac{1}{5}$ of a number is 30. What is the number?   *Ans* $= \ldots$

20. Take 4.73 from 8.

Ans = ...

21.   0.708

    × 1.2
    ———

    ———

22.   0.738 ÷ 9

   = ...

23.   3.564 kg ÷ 6

   = ... kg

24. What is 15% of 340 m?   *Ans* = ...

In a certain Composite school there are 600 pupils. 30% of them are Seniors, 35% of them are Juniors and the other pupils are Infants.

25. What percentage of the pupils are Infants? *Ans* = ...

26. There are . . . Seniors at the school

27. There are . . . Juniors at the school

28. There are . . . Infants at the school

Complete:

29. 40 mm = ... cm

30. 96 mm = ... cm

31. 4.5 km = ... m

32. 2 m = ... cm

33. 3.5 m = ... cm

34. If 2 L of orange juice cost $4.50, how much would 7 L of the same orange juice cost?   *Ans* = $...

The sum of the ages of Janice and Harriet is 52 years. Harriet is 6 years younger than Janice.

35. Harriet is . . . years old   **36.** Janice is . . . years old

Use each digit from here (3, 2, 9, 6) once only to write down:

37. The largest possible even number.   *Ans* = ...

38. The smallest possible odd number.   *Ans* = ...

39. Which of these numbers is not a multiple of 6?

    (3, 6, 12, 18, 24)   *Ans* = ...

40. Which factor of 12 is missing from these numbers?

    (6, 2, 1, 4, 3)   *Ans* = ...

41. Which of these numbers is not a prime number?

(2, 3, 5, 7, 9, 11)   *Ans* = ...

42. The length of a rectangle is 3 times as long as its width. If the length is 48 cm, what is the perimeter of the rectangle?   *Ans* = ... cm

If A = {Factors of 6} and B = {Odd numbers less than 6}:

43. $A \cup B$ = ...   **44.** $A \cap B$ = ...

A bus travels at 45 km per hour:

45. How long would it take to travel 135 km at the same rate?   *Ans* = ... h

46. How far would it travel in 24 min?   *Ans* = ... km

The diagram shows the favourite game of 36 pupils from Class 4. Two pupils like chess as their favourite game.

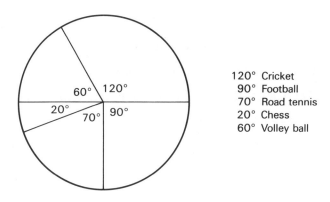

120° Cricket
90° Football
70° Road tennis
20° Chess
60° Volley ball

47. Which game is the most popular among the pupils?
                    Ans = ...

48. How many pupils like tennis as their favourite game?
                    Ans = ...

49. What fraction of the class like football?   *Ans* = ...

50. How many pupils like volleyball as their favourite game?
                    Ans = ...

Paper **15**

1. $1605 - 750 = \ldots$

2. $650 \times 8 = \ldots$

3.
$$
\begin{array}{r}
479 \\
\times\ 70 \\
\hline
\\
\hline
\end{array}
$$

4. $4015 \div 27 = \ldots$

5.
$$
\begin{array}{cc}
\$ & ¢ \\
\end{array}
$$
$84.36 \div 12 = \ldots$

6.
m	cm
3	46
2	97
+	84

7. The difference between two numbers is 48. The bigger number is 65. What is the other number? *Ans* $= \ldots$

8. A bucket when full holds $12\frac{1}{2}$ L of water. How many half-litres of water would it take to fill the bucket?

    Ans $= \ldots$

9. $\frac{3}{5} + \frac{1}{2} + \frac{1}{3} = \ldots$

10. $\frac{2}{3} \times \frac{3}{8} = \ldots$

11. $\frac{1}{4} \div 8 = \ldots$

12. One third of a number is 18. What is the number?

    Ans $= \ldots$

There are 60 plants in a garden. $\frac{1}{3}$ of them are crotons, $\frac{1}{6}$ of them are lilies and the rest are hibiscus.

13. How many plants are crotons? *Ans* $= \ldots$

14. How many plants are lilies? *Ans* $= \ldots$

15. How many plants are hibiscus? *Ans* $= \ldots$

16. $6.43 - 0.96 = \ldots$

17. $0.643 \times 0.06 = \ldots$

18. $15.2 \div 0.05 = \ldots$

19. A farmer sells his grade one eggs at $4.20 per box. If each box contains 12 eggs, what is the average price per egg?

Ans = $\ldots$

From the table below, calculate the time taken by a bus for each trip:

	Departure	*Arrival*	*Time taken* h *min*
20.	08 : 00	08 : 45	. . .
21.	09 : 25	10 : 20	. . .
22.	11 : 55	12 : 40	. . .
23.	13 : 05	14 : 00	. . .
24.	16 : 20	17 : 30	. . .
25.	20 : 50	21 : 40	. . .

Divide 186 marbles between Don and André so that Don gets twice as many as André.

26. Don gets . . . marbles   **27.** André gets . . . marbles

What are the coordinates of each letter in the diagram to the right?

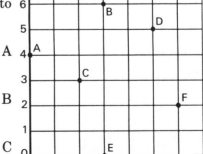

28. The coordinates of A = (. . .)

29. The coordinates of B = (. . .)

30. The coordinates of C = (. . .)

31. The coordinates of D = (. . .)

32. The coordinates of E = (. . .)

33. The coordinates of F = (. . .)

Calculate the value of the angles marked with letters. Angles marked with the same letter are equal.

34.

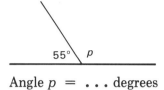

Angle p = ... degrees

35.

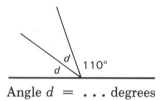

Angle d = ... degrees

36.

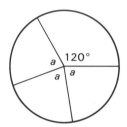

Angle a = ... degrees

37. Sugar is put in small bags each holding 2.5 kg. How many small bags can be filled from a large container which contains 90 kg? *Ans* = ...

If $m = 3, n = 2, p = 1$ and $q = 0$, find the value of:

38. $m + 3n$ = ...

39. $m \times n \times p \times q$ = ...

40. $m^2 - p^3$ = ...

41. $mn - pq$ = ...

42. $4mn^2 + 4m^2n$ = ...

43. List the set of factors of 16. *Ans* = ...

44. List the multiples of 6 between 1 and 40. *Ans* = ...

45. The sum of 3 consecutive odd numbers is 105. What are the 3 numbers? *Ans* = ...

46. What is the square root of 400? *Ans* = ...

The diagram below is drawn to a scale of 1 cm = 10 m.

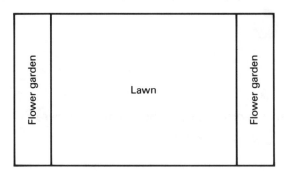

47. What is the length of the lawn? *Ans* = ... m

48. What is the width of the lawn? *Ans* = ... m

49. What is the area of the lawn? *Ans* = ... m²

50. What is the area of each flower garden? *Ans* = ... m²

Paper **16**

Complete the expansion for numbers written in base 8:

1. $276_8 = 2 \times 8^2 + 7 \times 8 + 6 \times \ldots$

2. $3054_8 = 3 \times 8^3 + 0 \times 8^2 + 5 \times \ldots + 4 \times 1$

3. $6517_8 = 6 \times \ldots + 5 \times 8^2 + 1 \times 8 + 7 \times 1$

Write in figures:

4. Fifty-two thousand three hundred.   *Ans* = ...

5. Six hundred and ten thousand and eight.   *Ans* = ...

Write in words:

6. 12 050   *Ans* = ...   **7.** 210 106   *Ans* = ...

8. A raffle book contained 40 tickets. Tickets numbered from 6 to 11 were not sold. How many tickets were sold?

9. $5026 \div 7$ = ...

11. $1472 \div 23$ = ...

10.
$$325 \times 73$$

Write as decimals:

12. $\dfrac{9}{100} = \ldots$ **13.** $\dfrac{76}{1000} = \ldots$ **14.** $\dfrac{3}{5} = \ldots$

15. From 10.0 take 7.63.   *Ans* = ...

16. $24 \div 0.5 = \ldots$

17. Divide 2.6 kg by 8.   *Ans* = ...kg

18. A piece of rope 6.65 m long is cut into 7 equal lengths. What does each length measure?   *Ans* = ...m

Our school bought 2500 exercise books at 40¢ each and sold them to the pupils at 50¢ each.

19. How much did the school pay for the books? *Ans* = $...

20. How much did the school collect for selling the 2500 books?   *Ans* = $...

21. How much profit did the school make?   *Ans* = $...

22. What was the school's percentage profit?   *Ans* = ...%

23. $3\frac{1}{5} \times 2\frac{1}{2} = $ ...   **24.** $2\frac{2}{3} \div 5\frac{1}{3} = $ ...

Use a sign from here ($<$, $=$, $>$), one in each space, to make correct statements:

25. $3 + 9 \ldots 72 \div 6$ **27.** $7 \times 0 \ldots 6 - 0$

26. $8 \times 8 \ldots 8 + 8$ **28.** $3^2 \ldots 5^2$

29. The perimeter of a rectangular piece of card is 84 cm. If the length of the card is 30 cm, what is the width?

$Ans = \ldots$ cm

Find the value of:

30. $12 - 2 \times 6 = $ ...

31. $8 \times 7 + 9 = $ ...

32. $17 \times 4 + 6 \times 13 = $ ...

33. $6 + 3 \times 4 + 11 = $ ...

34. $(8 + 6) \times 7 = $ ...

35. $16 \div 2 + 4 \times 7 = $ ...

36. Four similar rulers cost $1.20. What is the cost of 7 of these rulers?   *Ans* = $...

37. The average of 4 numbers is 50. Three of these numbers are 26, 73 and 39. What is the fourth number?

$Ans = \ldots$

List the following sets of numbers:

38. {First 5 prime numbers}   *Ans* = ...

39. {Odd numbers between 1 and 10}   *Ans* = ...

40.   {Multiples of 6 between 1 and 25}   *Ans* = ...

41.   {Factors of 18}   *Ans* = ...

42.   {First 6 whole numbers}   *Ans* = ...

The Express bus travels at an average speed of 60 km per hour.

43.   How far will it travel in $2\frac{1}{2}$ h?   *Ans* = ... km

44.   How long will it take to travel 240 km?   *Ans* = ... h

Calculate the value of the angles marked with letters. Angles marked with the same letters are equal.

45.

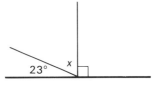

Angle x = ... degrees

46.

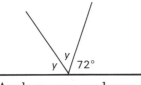

Angle y = ... degrees

47.

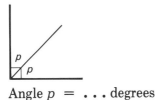

Angle p = ... degrees

48.

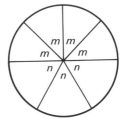

Angle m = ... degrees

49.   Angle n = ... degrees

The volume of a cuboid = length × width × height.

50.   Find the volume of a cuboid which is 8 cm long, 6 cm wide and 5 cm high.   *Ans* = ... cm^3

Paper **17**

Write the missing number in each series:

1. | 70, | 68, | 64, | 58, | . . . |

2. | 56, | 67, | 78, | . . . |

3. | 100, | 81, | 64, | 49, | . . . |

4. | 7.04, | 7.06, | 7.08, | . . . |

5. | 10, | 11, | 13, | 16, | . . . |

6. $5073 - 885 = \ldots$

7.
$$\begin{array}{r} 809 \\ \times \quad 7 \\ \hline \\ \hline \end{array}$$

8. $4788 \div 42 = \ldots$

9. Twelve times a number plus 4 equals 136. What is the number? $\qquad Ans = \ldots$

10. $\frac{5}{6} + \frac{3}{4} = \ldots$ **11.** $\frac{5}{8} \div 1\frac{3}{4} = \ldots$

12. What is $\frac{3}{4}$ of 300 kg? $\qquad Ans = \ldots$ kg

13. $\frac{2}{3}$ of a number is 60. What is the number? $Ans = \ldots$

Write the following decimals as fractions in their lowest terms:

14. $0.04 = \ldots$ **15.** $0.6 = \ldots$ **16.** $0.375 = \ldots$

17. $5.72 \times 1.2 = \ldots$ **18.** $0.097 \times 0.08 = \ldots$

19. When Mr Tyrell milked his cows he got 40.5 L of milk. He put the milk in containers each holding 1.5 L. How many containers were required? $\qquad Ans = \ldots$

Complete:

20. $55\% = \dfrac{}{40}$ **21.** $12\frac{1}{2}\% = \dfrac{}{8}$

22. What is 5% of 2 km?   *Ans* = ...m

Use two signs from here (+, −, ×, ÷), one in each space, to make correct statements:

23. 12...3 = 1...9

24. 16...4 = 8...8

25. 9...0 = 6...6

26. 24...3 = 6...2

27. 17...15 = 1...1

28. 6...13 = 21...2

29. Our school programme began at 14:30 hours and lasted for 1 h and 40 min. At what time did it finish?

               Ans = ...h...min

30. André was born on 5th May, 1973. On what date will he be 16 years and 9 months old?   *Ans* = ...

31. Mother bought a box of biscuits for $13.25 and 1 kg of cheese for $5.85. What change would she receive if she had given the cashier $20.00?   *Ans* = $...

Find the area of each triangle below:

32.

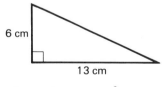

6 cm

13 cm

Area = ... cm^2

33.

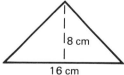

8 cm

16 cm

Area = ... cm^2

34.

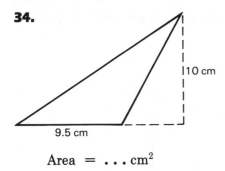

10 cm

9.5 cm

Area = ... cm^2

35. The area of a square is 256 cm^2. What is its perimeter?

Ans = ... cm

36. How much Canadian currency is equivalent to BB $74.00, if Can $1.00 = BB $1.48? Ans = Can $...

Solve the following equations:

37. $16 - a = 4$ $\therefore$ $a = $ ...

38. $2 \times p + 3 = 29$ $\therefore$ $p = $ ...

39. $m \times m = 36$ $\therefore$ $m = $ ...

40. $t + t + 5 = 23$ $\therefore$ $t = $ ...

41. $d - 9 = 13$ $\therefore$ $d = $ ...

42. $\dfrac{40}{n} = 5$ $\therefore$ $n = $ ...

43. The average number of men in 2 groups is 34. If 10 men leave one of the groups, what is the new average of the two groups? Ans = ...

Our school bought a colour TV for $600.00 and sold it at a loss of 10%.

44. How much did the school sell the TV for? Ans = $...

45. The sum of 3 consecutive numbers is 81. What are the 3 numbers? Ans = ...

The graph shows the marks obtained by the school's head girl in her six best subjects.

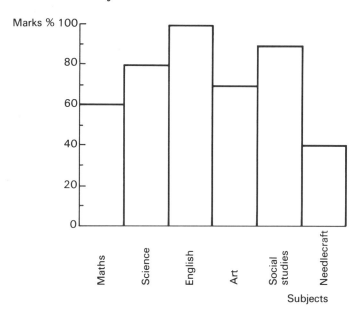

46. What percentage did she get in science?   *Ans* = ... %

47. In which subject did she get 100%?   *Ans* = ...

48. How many more marks did she get in social studies than in art?   *Ans* = ...

49. In which subject did she get below half marks?

   Ans = ...

50. What was the average for her 4 highest marks?

   Ans = ...

Paper **18**

Write in figures:

1. Fifteen thousand, six hundred and ten. *Ans* = ...

2. Eighty thousand and seven. *Ans* = ...

3. Six thousand and ten dollars and five cents. *Ans* = ...

Write in words:

4. 20 065 *Ans* = ... **6.** 110 420 *Ans* = ...

5. 31 006 *Ans* = ...

Change the following base 2 numbers to base 10 numbers:

7. $1\,1\,1_2$ = ... **9.** $1\,0\,1\,1_2$ = ...

8. $1\,1\,1\,0_2$ = ... **10.** $1\,1\,0\,1_2$ = ...

11. $3076 + 86 + 738$ **13.** $\begin{array}{r} 470 \\ \times\,386 \\ \hline \\ \hline \end{array}$

= ...

12. $8036 - 740$ = ... **14.** $3738 \div 29$

= ...

15. How many times can 12 be taken from 7224? *Ans* = ...

16. Last Saturday, Romeo picked 520 mangoes and Mark picked 26 fewer mangoes. How many mangoes did they pick in all? *Ans* = ...

17. A minibus started its journey with 35 passengers. During the journey, 26 passengers got off and 18 got on. How many passengers were on the bus at the end of the journey? *Ans* = ...

Look at the worked problem below and use it to help you give answers to the questions that follow:

$$\begin{array}{r} 68 \\ \times\,26 \\ \hline 1360 \\ 408 \\ \hline 1768 \end{array}$$

18. $1768 \div 26 = \ldots$

19. $1768 \div 68 = \ldots$

20. $34 \times 26 = \ldots$

21. $68 \times 52 = \ldots$

22. $68 \times 20 + 68 \times 6 = \ldots$

23. $68 \times 26 - 68 \times 6 = \ldots$

24. Angela had $10.00 in her purse, made up of 10¢ pieces and 25¢ pieces. If she had twenty 25¢ pieces, how many 10¢ pieces did she have?   *Ans* = ...

25. David began his homework at 18:30 hours. He spent 2 h and 45 min on it. At what time did he finish?

Ans = ...

26. $\frac{9}{12} - \frac{3}{8} = \ldots$ **27.** $\frac{5}{6} \times 3\frac{1}{5} = \ldots$

A fisherman caught 1500 flying fish. He sold $\frac{3}{5}$ of them to the villagers and the rest to a hotel.

28. What fraction did he sell to the hotel?   *Ans* = ...

29. How many fish did he sell to the hotel?   *Ans* = ...

30. How many fish did he sell to the villagers? *Ans* = ...

31. $6 + 15.9 + 9.85 = \ldots$ **32.** $0.420 \div 1.2 = \ldots$

33. What is $\frac{1}{8}$ of $100.00?   *Ans* = $...

34. How many pieces of rope each measuring 2.5 m can be cut from a piece of rope measuring 47.5 m? *Ans* = ...

If $A = \{1, 2, 3, 4, 5\}, B = \{1, 3, 5, 7, 9\}$ and $C = \{2, 3, 5, 7\}$, list:

35. $B \cap C = \ldots$

38. $B \cup C = \ldots$

36. $A \cap C = \ldots$

39. $A \cup C = \ldots$

37. $A \cup B = \ldots$

40. $900 = 2 \times 2 \times 3 \times 3 \times 5 \times 5$. What is the square root of 900? *Ans* $= \ldots$

3 lambs are worth the same as 2 piglets.

41. 24 lambs are worth . . . piglets

42. 10 piglets are worth . . . lambs

43. How many piglets can be exchanged for 45 lambs?

Ans $= \ldots$

In each of the following equations find the value of each letter:

44. $x + 13 = 20 \quad \therefore \quad x = \ldots$

45. $m - 8 = 15 \quad \therefore \quad m = \ldots$

46. $19 - n = 11 \quad \therefore \quad n = \ldots$

47. $a + a + 3 = 27 \quad \therefore \quad a = \ldots$

48. $4 \times y - 6 = 42 \quad \therefore \quad y = \ldots$

49. $d \times d + 3 = 67 \quad \therefore \quad d = \ldots$

50. What is the area of the shaded part of the square below?

Ans $= \ldots \text{cm}^2$

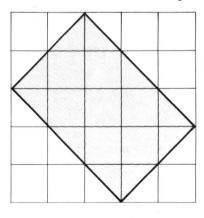

Paper **19**

1. $47.65 + $268.40 + $95.88 = $...

2. $310.00 − $75.82 = $...

3. $163.80 ÷ 9 = $...

4.　　568
　　× 80
　　‾‾‾‾‾

　　　‾‾‾‾‾

5.　　718
　　× 53
　　‾‾‾‾‾

　　　‾‾‾‾‾

6. 1588 ÷ 19 = ...

7. Ten trees are planted in a straight line, equal distances apart. If the distance between any two successive trees is 8 m, what is the distance between the first and tenth trees?　　　　　*Ans* = ... m

8. A box contains 85 candies. Find the cost of 5 similar boxes of candies if 1 candy costs 12 ¢.　*Ans* = $...

Complete:

9. $\dfrac{4}{15} = \dfrac{}{30}$　　10. $\dfrac{1}{} = \dfrac{9}{45}$　　11. $\dfrac{5}{6} = \dfrac{2\times}{24}$

12. $\frac{1}{3} + \frac{1}{2} + \frac{3}{4} = $ ...　　14. $3\frac{2}{3} \times \frac{2}{15} = $ ...

13. $3\frac{1}{2} - 1\frac{7}{8} = $ ...　　15. $\frac{3}{8} \div 2\frac{1}{4} = $ ...

16. $\frac{1}{6}$ of a number is 24. What is the number?　*Ans* = ...

17. 16 − 3.07 = ...　　18. 2.87 × 0.09 = ...

19. 46 ÷ 0.05 = ...

20. A boy's average step measures 0.8 m. How many steps would he take to walk 1 km?　　*Ans* = ...

Complete:

21. 3 h = ... min

22. 240 s = ... min

23. min s

     9 16

  ×   8

  ―――――

24.   h   min

   7 ⟌ 78   3

   = ...

25. It takes Joan 40 min to complete a piece of needlecraft. If she begins work at 10:30 hours, at what time will she complete 6 similar pieces of needlecraft?   *Ans* = ...

Complete the diagrams below to make the line MN a line of symmetry:

26.

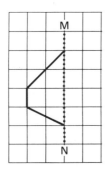

27.

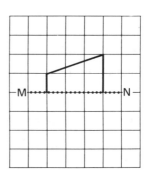

28.

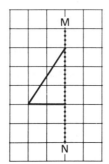

29.

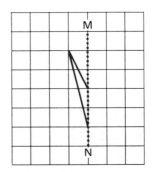

The graph below shows the different ways by which all the pupils from our class come to school.

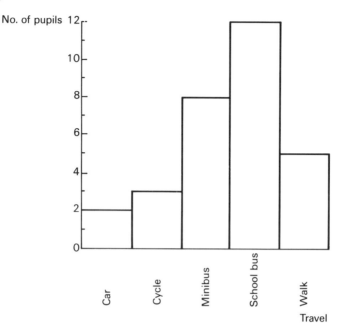

30. How many pupils come to school by minibus

Ans = ...

31. How many pupils walk to school?   *Ans* = ...

32. Which is the most popular way of coming to school?

Ans = ...

33. How many pupils are in our class?   *Ans* = ...

34. What percentage of the pupils come to school by cycle?

Ans = ... %

35. What is 25% of $1000.00?   *Ans* = $...

36. In 4 innings a cricketer had scores of 40, 67, 19 and 109. How many runs does he need to score in the fifth innings to have an average of 50?   *Ans* = ...

Find the value of the following:

37. $2 \times 2 \times 2 \times 3 \times 3$ = ...

38. $2^4 + 4^2$ = ...

39. $5^2 + 4^2 = \dots$

40. $5 \times 8 + 3 \times 12 = \dots$

41. $8 \times (3 + 9) \div 6 = \dots$

Plot the following points in the diagram to the right. R(5, 2) is already plotted as an example.

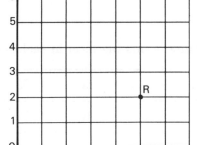

42. A(5, 1)

43. B(7, 3)

44. C(3, 4)

45. D(2, 0)

46. E(0, 6)

The length of a rectangle is twice its width. If the perimeter is 72 cm, what is the measurement of:

47. The width.   *Ans* = ... cm

48. The length.   *Ans* = ... cm

49. Its area.   *Ans* = ... cm^2

50. Five pairs of socks cost \$25.00. Find the cost of 8 pairs of similar socks.   *Ans* = \$...

Paper 20

Write the missing term in each series:

1.	60,	56,	52,	. . .	
2.	15,	16,	18,	21,	. . .
3.	125,	64,	27,	8,	. . .
4.	87,	76,	65,	. . .	
5.	1×3,	2×5,	3×7,	4×9,	. . .

6. $1377 \div 9 = \ldots$ **8.** $7450 \div 25 = \ldots$

7. $4860 \div 30 = \ldots$ **9.** $3207 - 809 = \ldots$

10.
$$483$$
$$\times \, 607$$
———
———

11.
$$745$$
$$\times \, 60$$
———
———

12. $2\frac{1}{4} - 1\frac{5}{8} = \ldots$ **13.** $3\frac{1}{3} \div 1\frac{4}{5} = \ldots$

14. What is $\frac{3}{8}$ of 720?   *Ans* $= \ldots$

15. $32.76 - 9.8 = \ldots$ **16.** $0.954 \div 0.9 = \ldots$

Only 45% of our school children have visited Harrison's Cave.

17. What percentage of our school children have not visited the cave?   *Ans* $= \ldots \%$

18. If there are 400 pupils at our school, how many have visited the cave?   *Ans* $= \ldots$

Change the following measurements to metres:

19. 400 cm = ... m   **20.** 1200 cm = ... m

Below is part of a calendar for the month of August:

Sun.	Mon.	Tue.	Wed.	Thurs.	Fri.	Sat.
		20	21	22	23	24
25	26	27	28	29	30	31

Study this part of the calendar and then answer the questions below:

21. How many Saturdays are there in the month of August?

Ans = ...

22. On what day of the week did the month of August begin?

Ans = ...

23. On what date was the first Tuesday in August?

Ans = ...

24. What day of the week was the 3rd of August? *Ans* = ...

Use two signs from here (+, −, ×, ÷), one in each space, to make each statement correct:

25. 6 ... 4 ... 8 = 16

26. 12 ... 12 ... 7 = 7

27. (3 ... 2) ... 4 = 20

28. 6 ... $\frac{1}{2}$ ... 2 = 5

29. 2 ... 2 ... 2 = 8

30. (8 ... 8) ... 5 = 0

A cyclist travels at an average speed of 20 km per hour:

31. How far does he travel in 45 min at the same rate?

Ans = ... km

32. How long does he take to travel 90 km at the same rate?

Ans = ... h

Calculate the value of each letter in the following diagrams.
Angles marked with the same letter are equal.

33.

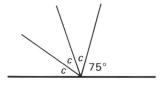

Angle c = ... degrees

34.

35.

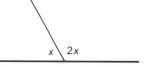

Angle x = ... degrees

Angle $2x$ = ... degrees

36.

37.

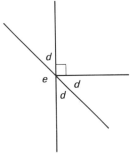

Angle d = ... degrees

Angle e = ... degrees

The area of a rectangle is $144\,\text{cm}^2$. If the length is $16\,\text{cm}$, calculate:

38.   The width.   *Ans* = ... cm

39.   The perimeter.   *Ans* = ... cm

Use each digit from here (7, 2, 3, 8) once only to form

40.   The smallest possible even number.   *Ans* = ...

41.   The smallest possible odd number.   *Ans* = ...

42.   The largest possible even number.   *Ans* = ...

43.   The largest possible odd number.   *Ans* = ...

In the diagram to the right

G = {Girls who run the 100 m}

R = {Girls who run the 200 m}

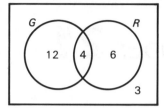

44. How many girls run the 100 m?   *Ans* = . . .

45. How many girls run the 200 m?   *Ans* = . . .

46. How many girls run both the 100 m and the 200 m?

Ans = . . .

47. How many girls run neither the 100 m nor the 200 m?

Ans = . . .

The diagram below shows the plan of the floor of a room drawn to a scale of 1 cm = 2 m.

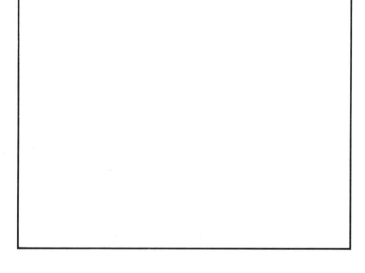

48. The length of the room = . . . m

49. The width of the room = . . . m

50. The area of the room = . . . m^2

Paper **21**

In the following numbers put in a decimal point to make the 4 equal to 4 tens:

1. 74 159 = ...

3. 45 917 = ...

2. 95 471 = ...

4. 591 470 = ...

Solve the following equations:

5. $t - 5 = 13$ ∴ $t = $ ...

6. $3x = 36$ ∴ $x = $ ...

7. $p \times 4 + 3 = 31$ ∴ $p = $ ...

8. $a + a + a = 27$ ∴ $a = $ ...

9. $m \times m = 121$ ∴ $m = $ ...

10. $16 = \dfrac{n}{8}$ ∴ $n = $ ...

11.
$$\begin{array}{r} 1408 \\ \times \quad 76 \\ \hline \\ \hline \end{array}$$

12. 10 829 ÷ 17

= ...

13. Subtract

h	min
23	10
− 15	45

14. $\frac{5}{6} + \frac{3}{4} = $ ...

15. $\frac{7}{8} - \frac{1}{2} = $ ...

16. $\frac{7}{15} \times \frac{5}{14} = $ ...

17. $4\frac{2}{3} \div 3\frac{1}{3} = $ ...

18. $18.07 + 6.42 - 9.683 = $ ...

19. $5.97 \times 0.08 = $ ...

20. $0.6318 \div 9 = \ldots$

21. A farmer wanted 35 L of milk from his 3 cows. The first cow gave 12.5 L and the second gave 9.75 L. How much does the third cow need to give? *Ans* = $\ldots$ L

22. What is 12% of $25.50? *Ans* = $\ldots

23. 15% of our church members are vegetarians. What percentage are not vegetarians? *Ans* = $\ldots$ %

From this set of numbers $\{23, 25, 27, 29, 31, 33, 35, 37, 39\}$, find:

24. The smallest prime number. *Ans* = $\ldots$

25. The largest prime number. *Ans* = $\ldots$

26. The number which is a multiple of 9. *Ans* = $\ldots$

27. The average of these numbers. *Ans* = $\ldots$

Use a sign from here ($<$, $=$, $>$) in each space to make each statement true:

28. $9 + 3 \ldots 16 - 5$ **31.** $2^3 \ldots 3^2$

29. $7 \times 8 \ldots 9 \times 6$ **32.** $1 \times 1 \times 1 \ldots 1 + 2$

30. $8 \times 0 \ldots 16 \div 16$

33. Find the area of the shaded triangle to the right. *Ans* = $\ldots$ cm^2

8 cm

12 cm

The diagram to the right shows the plan of a plot of land drawn to a scale of 1 cm = 10 m. By using a ruler and calculations find the measurements of:

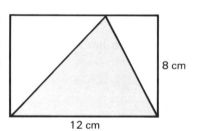

34. AB = $\ldots$ m   **36.** DC = $\ldots$ m

35. BC = $\ldots$ m

37. The distance from A to C in a straight line $= \ldots$ m

38. What is the area of the plot of land? $Ans = \ldots$ m^2

81 expressed as a product of prime factors $= 3 \times 3 \times 3 \times 3$.

$\therefore$ the square root of 81 $= 3 \times 3 = 9$.

Express the following numbers as products of prime factors:

39. $64 = \ldots$ **41.** $144 = \ldots$

40. $100 = \ldots$ **42.** $196 = \ldots$

What is the square root of:

43. $64 = \ldots$ **45.** $144 = \ldots$

44. $100 = \ldots$ **46.** $196 = \ldots$

Divide 270 mangoes into 2 shares in the ratio $4 : 5$.

47. One share $= \ldots$ mangoes

48. The other share $= \ldots$ mangoes

49. If 4 water coconuts cost \$3.00, find the cost of 10 water coconuts at the same rate. $Ans = \$\ldots$

50. David had p sheep. His friend John had 5 fewer sheep than David. Write down an expression for the number of sheep John had. $Ans = \ldots$

Paper 22

Complete:

1. $68 \times 46 + 81 \times 46 = \ldots \times 46$

2. $571 = 57 \times \ldots + 1 \times 1$

3. $43 \times 270 = 43 \times 200 + 43 \times \ldots$

Write in figures:

4. Seventeen thousand and eleven.   *Ans* = ...

5. Two hundred and five thousand and fifty.   *Ans* = ...

Write in words:

6. $10\,060 = \ldots$

7. $410\,715 = \ldots$

8. $7051 - 3682 = \ldots$

9.   387   **10.**   361

      $\times\ 50$ $\times\ 84$

11. How many times can 25 be taken from 7550? *Ans* = ...

12. $1\frac{1}{3} + 2\frac{3}{4} = \ldots$ **14.** $5\frac{1}{3} \times 1\frac{1}{5} = \ldots$

13. $3\frac{1}{2} - 2\frac{2}{3} = \ldots$ **15.** $\frac{3}{8} \div 2\frac{2}{3} = \ldots$

16. What is $\frac{3}{4}$ of \$150?   *Ans* = \$...

17. $\frac{1}{5}$ of a number is 15. What is the number?   *Ans* = ...

18. Michael had a bar of chocolate. He ate $\frac{1}{2}$ of it and gave away $\frac{1}{3}$. What fraction had he left?   *Ans* = ...

19. $5.0 - 2.75 + 0.95 = \ldots$ **21.** $31.56 \div 6 = \ldots$

20. $6.27 \times 0.9 = \ldots$ **22.** $4.2 \div 0.8 = \ldots$

23. A loaf of bread weighs 0.09 kg. What is the weight of 18 loaves of bread?   *Ans* = ...g

Complete:

24. $\frac{16}{25}$ = ...%   **25.** $\frac{24}{60}$ = ...%   **26.** $\frac{6}{5}$ = ...%

27. What is 25% of 2 kg?   *Ans* = ...g

500 pupils wrote a certain examination. If 60% of these pupils passed the exam:

28. What percentage of the pupils failed?   *Ans* = ...%

29. How many pupils failed?   *Ans* = ...

30. How many pupils passed?   *Ans* = ...

31. Add

$	¢
47	65
168	09
+ 46	71

33. Multiply

m	cm
5	67
×	8

32. Subtract

h	min
28	25
− 8	40

34. How many 5¢ pieces are worth the same as fifteen 25¢ pieces?   *Ans* = ...

35. The first lesson at our school lasted for 80 min and finished at 10.05 a.m. At what time did it begin?

                    Ans = ...

The perimeter of a rectangle is 84 cm. If the width is half as long as the length, calculate the following.

36. The length of the rectangle.   *Ans* = ...cm

37.   The width of the rectangle = ...cm

38.   The area of the rectangle = ...cm²

If $m = 2$, $n = 1$ and $p = 0$, find the value of:

39. $m + 3n = ...$ **41.** $mn - np = ...$

40. $m \times n \times p = ...$ **42.** $m^2 + n^2 = ...$

43.   List all the factors of 28   *Ans* = ...

Study the diagram below and then answer the questions that follow.

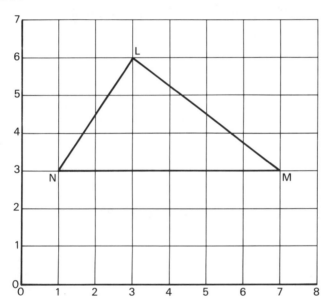

44.   What are the coordinates of L?   *Ans* = (...)

45.   What are the coordinates of M?   *Ans* = (...)

46.   What are the coordinates of N?   *Ans* = (...)

47.   What kind of triangle is this?   *Ans* = ...

48.   The area of triangle LMN = ...cm²

Divide 120 golden apples between Ann and Pam so that Ann gets 8 more than Pam.

49.   Ann gets ... golden apples

50.   Pam gets ... golden apples

Paper **23**

1. $6743 - 5847 = \ldots$

2. Find the sum of 76, 2076 and 987.   *Ans* $= \ldots$

3. What is the difference between 607 and 390? *Ans* $= \ldots$

4. The sum of two numbers is 565. If one number is 275, what is the other?   *Ans* $= \ldots$

5. 678×7
$= \ldots$

6. $\begin{array}{r} 509 \\ \times\ 40 \\ \hline \\ \hline \end{array}$

7. $\begin{array}{r} 370 \\ \times\ 84 \\ \hline \\ \hline \end{array}$

8. $8464 \div 8$
$= \ldots$

9. $2750 \div 50$
$= \ldots$

10. $7696 \div 37$
$= \ldots$

11. The product of two numbers is 144. If one number is 9, what is the other number?   *Ans* $= \ldots$

Complete the following correctly:

12. $467 = 4$ hundreds $+ \ldots$ tens $+ 7$ ones

13. $258 = \ldots$ tens $+ 8$ ones

14. $1740 = \ldots$ hundreds $+ 4$ tens

15. $2076 = 2$ thousands $+ \ldots$ ones

Complete the following correctly:

16. $\dfrac{3}{8} = \dfrac{}{40}$

19. $\frac{3}{5} + \frac{1}{4} = \ldots$

17. $\dfrac{}{5} = \dfrac{15}{25}$

20. $\frac{7}{8} - \frac{3}{4} = \ldots$

18. $\dfrac{3}{4} = \dfrac{2 \times}{24}$

21. $\frac{7}{10} \times 1\frac{2}{3} = \ldots$

22. $8 \div \frac{1}{2} = \ldots$

23. What is $\frac{2}{5}$ of 40?   *Ans* $= \ldots$

The boys from our class reaped 75 kg of cucumbers from the school garden. They sold $\frac{1}{3}$ of them to the teachers and $\frac{2}{5}$ to a minimart.

24. What fraction of the cucumbers was left?   *Ans* $= \ldots$
25. How much was sold to the teachers?   *Ans* $= \ldots$ kg
26. How much was sold to the minimart?   *Ans* $= \ldots$ kg
27. How much was left?   *Ans* $= \ldots$ kg
28. One sixth $\left(\frac{1}{6}\right)$ of a number is 24. What is the number?

Ans $= \ldots$

In the number 805.61, which digit gives the number of:

29. tens . . .

32. tenths . . .

30. hundredths . . .

33. hundreds . . .

31. units . . .

Change to metres:

34. 600 cm $= \ldots$ m

36. 2.5 km $= \ldots$ m

35. 250 cm $= \ldots$ m

The graph below shows the attendance for Class 4 during one week. 30 pupils are in Class 4.

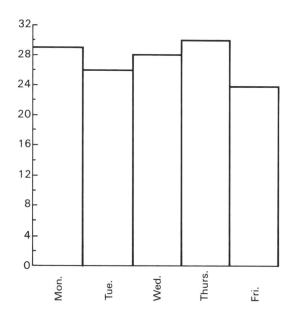

37. How many pupils came to school on Tuesday?

Ans = ...

38. How many pupils were absent on Wednesday?

Ans = ...

39. On which day did all the pupils come to school?

Ans = ...

40. What percentage of the pupils came to school on Friday?

Ans = ...%

41. What was the average attendance for the week?

Ans = ...

At the 'back to school sale' my mother paid $5.00 for a set containing books and pencils. If the books cost $1.50 more than the pencils, what was the cost of:

42. The books?   *Ans* = $...

43. The pencils?   *Ans* = $...

The length of our classroom is twice its width. If the length is 13 m, what is:

44.   The perimeter?   *Ans* = . . . cm

45.   The area?   *Ans* = . . . cm².

46.   The diameter of a circle is 14 cm. What is its radius?

Ans = . . . cm

US $1.00 is worth BB $1.98.

47.   How much Barbados currency is worth US $5.00?

Ans = BB $ . . .

48.   How much US currency is worth $39.60 in Barbados currency?   *Ans* = $ . . .

An angle of 65 degrees is an acute angle.

49.   An angle of 178 degrees is . . . angle

50.   An angle of 189 degrees is . . . angle

Paper 24

Write in figures:

1. Eighteen thousand and seven. *Ans* = ...

2. Two hundred thousand and twenty. *Ans* = ...

3. Five hundred and ten dollars and five cents. *Ans* = ...

4. Subtract

$$
\begin{array}{cc}
\$ & ¢ \\
437 & 50 \\
- \ 98 & 76 \\
\hline
\end{array}
$$

6.
$$
\begin{array}{r}
712 \\
\times \ 9 \\
\hline
\\
\hline
\end{array}
$$

5. Divide

$\$135.63 \div 9$

= ...

7.
$$
\begin{array}{r}
307 \\
\times \ 68 \\
\hline
\\
\hline
\end{array}
$$

8. What is $\frac{1}{8}$ of 4064? *Ans* = ...

Look at the worked problem and then use it to help you give answers to the questions that follow:

$$
\begin{array}{r}
76 \\
\times \ 48 \\
\hline
3040 \\
608 \\
\hline
3648 \\
\hline
\end{array}
$$

9. $3648 \div 76 = \ldots$

10. $3648 \div 48 = \ldots$

11. $76 \times 96 = \ldots$

12. $48 \times 38 = \ldots$

13. $75 \times 48 = \ldots$

14. $76 \times 40 + 76 \times 8 = \ldots$

15. $76 \times 48 - 76 \times 8 = \ldots$

16. How many times can 16 be taken from 1712? *Ans* $= \ldots$

17. $3\frac{1}{4} - 2\frac{7}{8} = \ldots$

18. $\frac{5}{6} \div \frac{2}{3} = \ldots$ **19.** $\frac{3}{4} \div 1\frac{4}{5} = \ldots$

20. How many quarters are in $6\frac{1}{4}$?   *Ans* $= \ldots$

In a class of 24 pupils, 6 were absent from school and 3 were attending the dentist.

21. What fraction of the pupils were absent from school?

Ans $= \ldots$

22. What fraction of the pupils were at the dentist?

Ans $= \ldots$

23. What fraction of the pupils were present?   *Ans* $= \ldots$

Here are five shapes. Choose names from here (triangle, rectangle, cylinder, sphere, circle, cuboid, cone) to identify them:

24.

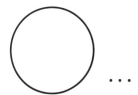

. . .

25.

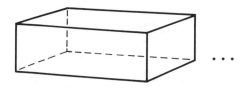

. . .

26.

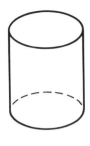

. . .

27.

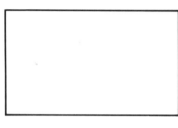

. . .

28.

. . .

29. $12 - 8.26 = $ . . .

30. $4.2 \times 1.2 = $ . . .

31. $4.65 \div 1.5 = $ . . .

A fishseller bought 600 flying fish at $18.00 per hundred. She sold them at 3 for $1.00.

32. How much did she pay for the 600 flying fish?

$$Ans = \$ \ldots$$

33. How much did she get for the 600 flying fish?

$$Ans = \$ \ldots$$

34. How much profit did she make? $Ans = \$ \ldots$

Use a sign from here (<, =, >) in each space to make each statement correct:

35. $15 - 4 \ldots 3 + 7$ **37.** $6 \times 8 \ldots 74 - 26$

36. $5^2 \ldots 2^5$ **38.** $1 \times 1 \ldots 2 \times 0$

39. If US $1.00 is worth BB $1.98, how much Barbados currency is worth US $12.00?   *Ans* = BB $ . . .

Complete:

40. $4\frac{1}{4}$ h = . . . min

41. $1\frac{3}{4}$ min = . . . s

42. 360 s = . . . min

43. A TV programme began at 19:30 hours and lasted for 1 h and 40 min. At what time did it finish?

                Ans = . . .

In the diagram to the right

S = {Factors of 6} and

E = {Factors of 8}

44. Six has . . . factors

45. Eight has . . . factors

46. How many factors of 6 are also factors of 8?

          Ans = . . .

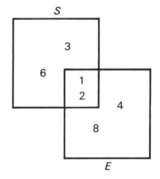

47. If 8 bananas cost $2.40, find the cost of 5 bananas at the same rate.   *Ans* = $ . . .

48. The diameter of a circle is 35 cm. What is its radius?

          Ans = . . . cm

A boy runs at an average speed of 8 km per hour.

49. How far can he run in 90 min?   *Ans* = . . . km

50. How long would it take him to run 28 km? *Ans* = . . . h

Paper 25

Write the missing numbers in each of the following series:

1.	8,	9,	11,	14,	. . .
2.	64,	59,	54,	. . .	
3.	0.25,	0.75,	1.25,	. . .	
4.	2,	1,	$\frac{1}{2}$,	$\frac{1}{4}$,	. . .
5.	16,	25,	36,	49,	. . .

6. The difference of two numbers is 67. If the larger number is 93, what is the smaller number? *Ans* = . . .

7. What is the remainder when 5001 is divided by 12? *Ans* = . . .

8. Multiply

```
   m    cm
   3    47
×        8
_____
```

9. Subtract

```
   cm    mm
   17     6
−   8     8
_____
```

10. Divide

kg

$3.605 \div 7$

= . . .

11. One third $\left(\frac{1}{3}\right)$ of a number is 18. What is the number? *Ans* = . . .

12. What is $\frac{2}{3}$ of 60 min? *Ans* = . . . min

Complete:

13. $\dfrac{3}{-} = \dfrac{15}{25}$

14. $\dfrac{7}{8} = \dfrac{}{40}$

15. $\dfrac{5}{6} = \dfrac{5 \times}{30}$

16. $\frac{3}{4} + \frac{2}{3} = \ldots$

17. $1\frac{1}{4} - \frac{7}{8} = \ldots$

18. $\frac{3}{10} \times \frac{8}{15} = \ldots$

19. $3\frac{1}{2} \div \frac{3}{4} = \ldots$

20. $\frac{16}{25} \div 1\frac{1}{5} = \ldots$

21. List the prime numbers between 20 and 30. *Ans* = $\ldots$

In each of the following equations, find the value of each letter:

22. $4 \times a = 36$

23. $17 - x = 12$

24. $m - 8 = 8$

25. $t \times t - 4 = 60$

26. $2 \times d + 7 = 31$

My father divided \$3.00 between my brother and me so that I got 10¢ more than my brother.

27. My brother got \$ . . .   **28.** I got \$ . . .

Use two signs from here ($+$, $-$, $\times$, $\div$), one in each space, to make each statement correct:

29. $(8 \ldots 6) \ldots 2 = 7$ **32.** $(9 \ldots 7) \ldots 4 = 4$

30. $12 \ldots 5 \ldots 3 = 10$ **33.** $4 \ldots 4 \ldots 2 = 10$

31. $3 \ldots 6 \ldots 9 = 2$

Study the diagram to the right and then write the coordinates of each letter. For example, the coordinates of P = (5, 3).

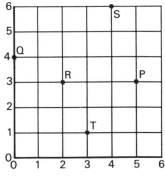

34. The coordinates of Q = (. . .)

35. The coordinates of R = (. . .)

36. The coordinates of S = (. . .)

37. The coordinates of T = (. . .)

38. The cash price of a hat is $30.00. If a discount of 10% is given for cash payments, what does a customer pay for the hat if he pays cash? *Ans* = $...

39. The radius of a circle is 12.5 cm. What is its diameter?

Ans = ... cm

40. $6.06 - 0.97 = ...$ **42.** $0.875 \times 0.04 = ...$

41. $18 + 6.7 + 0.95 = ...$ **43.** $0.476 \div 0.7 = ...$

Calculate the value of each letter in the following diagrams. Angles marked with the same letters are equal.

44. Angle a = ... degrees

45. Angle b = ... degrees

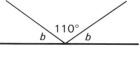

46. Angle c = ... degrees

47. Angle d = ... degrees

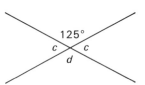

In the diagrams below estimate the areas of A and B, and calculate the area of C.

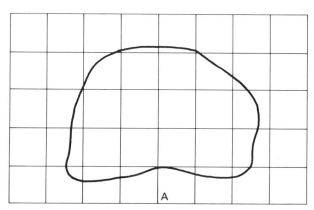

48. Area of A = ... cm^2

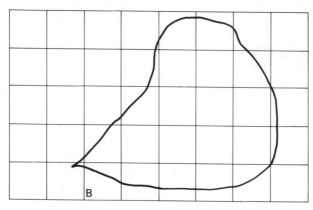

49. Area of B = . . . cm²

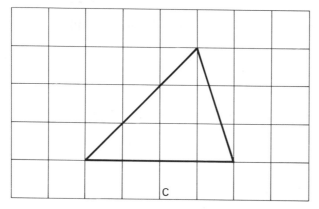

50. Area of C = . . . cm²

Test **One**

1. Add   234
        + 125
        ———

2. Subtract   646
          − 215
          ———

3. Multiply   203
          ×   3
          ———

4. Divide $4\overline{)840}$

5. $46 + 327 + 9 = \ldots$

6. Multiply   708
          ×   7
          ———

7. Write in words: 25 005   *Ans* = ...

8. Find the product of 72 and 6.   *Ans* = ...

9. The sum of two numbers is 108. If one number is 20, what is the other number?   *Ans* = ...

10. 8 times a certain number is 96. What is the number?

                               Ans = ...

Write the missing number in each series:

11.	10,	11,	13,	16,	...
12.	64,	49,	36,	25,	...
13.	4,	2,	1,	$\frac{1}{2}$,	...
14.	67,	78,	89,	...	

Complete the following correctly:

15. $48 \times 35 + 48 \times 25 = 48 \times \ldots$

16. $67 \times 49 - 67 \times 21 = 67 \times \ldots$

Write in figures:

17.   Ten thousand and forty.   *Ans* = $\ldots$

18. $\frac{1}{4}$ of my pocket money is $2.50. How much do I have for pocket money?   *Ans* = $\ldots$

19.   Divide

$4248 \div 6$

$= \ldots$

Use a sign from here $(<, =, >)$ in each space to make each statement true.

20. $12 - 3 \ldots 4 + 5$

21. $2 \times 2 \times 2 \ldots 2 + 2 + 2$

22. $16 \times 1 \ldots 16 - 0$

23. $3^2 \ldots 2^3$

24. $5 \times 0 \ldots 40 \div 8$

25.   What is 125% of 400 g?   *Ans* = $\ldots$ g

26.   Flying fish are sold at 6 for $1.00. How much would I have to pay for 21 flying fish at this price?   *Ans* = $\ldots$

Complete each statement correctly:

27. $\dfrac{3}{5} = \dfrac{}{20}$

28. $\dfrac{5}{8} = \dfrac{5 \times}{24}$

29. $\dfrac{7}{10} + \dfrac{1}{5} = \dfrac{}{10}$

30. $1\frac{1}{4} - \dfrac{2}{3} = \dfrac{}{12}$

31. $\dfrac{1}{6} \times 2\frac{1}{4} = \dfrac{}{8}$

32. $\dfrac{2}{3} \div \dfrac{3}{4} = \dfrac{}{}$

In the number 627.503, which digit stands for

33.   tenths $\ldots$

34.   hundredths $\ldots$

35.   tens $\ldots$

36.   ones $\ldots$

Use the following digits (5, 4, 7, 2) once only to form:

37. The largest possible number. *Ans* = ...

38. The smallest possible number. *Ans* = ...

39. The largest possible odd number. *Ans* = ...

40. The smallest possible even number. *Ans* = ...

What is the value of each letter in the following equations:

41. $A - 3 = 10$ A = ...

42. $B \times B = 64$ B = ...

43. $4 \times T = 4$ T = ...

44. $\dfrac{R}{4} = 12$ R = ...

45. $\dfrac{40}{M} = 4$ M = ...

46. Which number is not a factor of 12?
{1, 2, 3, 4, 6, 8, 12} *Ans* = ...

47. Which number is a multiple of 4?
{2, 6, 10, 16, 18} *Ans* = ...

48. Through how many degrees does the minute hand of a clock rotate in 20 min? *Ans* = ... degrees

In the figures below the angles marked with the same letter are equal.

49. What is the value of c?
Ans = ... degrees

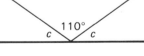

50. What is the value of y?
Ans = ... degrees

51. What is the value of x?
Ans = ... degrees

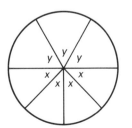

52. $\frac{3}{5}$ of the pupils in Class 4 are girls. If there are 15 girls, how many pupils are in Class 4? *Ans* = ...

53. How much Barbados currency is equivalent to US $30.00 if US $1.00 = BB $1.98? *Ans* = BB $. . .

54. Mrs Lucas bought 100 buns for $20.00. She sold them at 35¢ each. What was her profit? *Ans* = $. . .

55. At a sale a bicycle which usually costs $500.00 was reduced by 25%. How much must be paid for it?

Ans = $. . .

56. Find the area of the shaded part of the figure below:

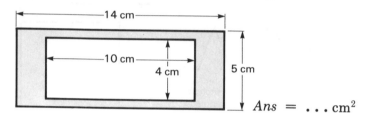

Ans = . . . cm²

57. The average of 3 numbers is 28 and the average of 4 numbers is 35. What is the average of the 7 numbers?

Ans = . . .

A cricketer scored 120 runs of which 75% were in boundaries.

58. What percentage were not in boundaries? *Ans* = . . . %

59. How many runs were in boundaries? *Ans* = . . .

Mother divided 105 plums between André and Akari so that André got twice as many as Akari.

60. André got . . . plums **61.** Akari got . . . plums

In the diagram below the coordinates of C are (5, 2).

62. The coordinates of A = (. . .)

63. The coordinates of B = (. . .)

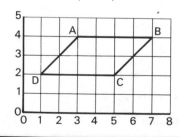

64. The area of figure ABCD = . . . cm^2

65. ABCD is a (square, rectangle, parallelogram, rhombus)

Ans = . . .

Look at the diagrams below:

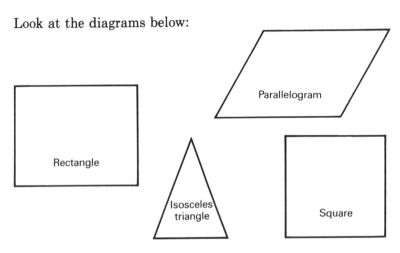

66. Which figure has no lines of symmetry?   *Ans* = . . .

67. Which figure has one line of symmetry?   *Ans* = . . .

68. Which figure has two lines of symmetry?   *Ans* = . . .

69. Which figure has four lines of symmetry?   *Ans* = . . .

70. At most, how many times can 17 be taken from 391?

Ans = . . .

Change to centimetres:

71. 240 mm = . . . cm   **72.** 15 m = . . . cm

The figure to the right is a cuboid.

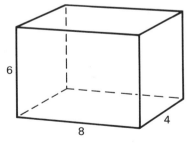

73. How many faces has it?

Ans = . . .

74. How many corners has it?   *Ans* = . . .

75. How many edges has it?

Ans = . . .

76. What is its volume?   *Ans* = . . . cm^3

The diagram below shows three sets *A, B* and *C* where each letter represents a member.

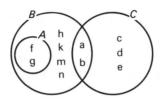

77. How many members are in set *B*?   *Ans* = ...

78. How many members are in set *C* only?   *Ans* = ...

79. How many members are in set *B* but neither in set *A* nor set *C*?   *Ans* = ...

80. How many members are in both set *B* and set *C*?

Ans = ...

81. How many members are in set *A* and also in set *B*?

Ans = ...

The express school bus travels at 48 km per hour.

82. How far would it travel in $2\frac{1}{2}$ h at this rate?

Ans = ...km

83. How long would it take to travel 240 km? *Ans* = ...h

The graph shows the times that were taken by 6 students to type 30 words.

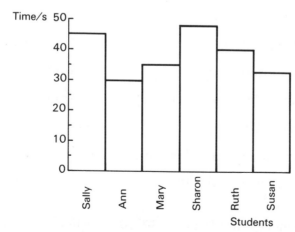

84. Who was the fastest typist?   *Ans* = ...

85.   Who was the slowest typist?   *Ans* = . . .

86.   Who took 35 s to type the words?   *Ans* = . . .

87.   How many students typed faster than Ruth?

Ans = . . .

88.   At this rate, how many words per minute can Sally type?

Ans = . . .

89.   How many bottles each holding 1.5 L can be filled from a container holding 15 L?   *Ans* = . . .

90.   My father left home at 7.30 a.m. and took 45 min to get to work. At what time did he arrive at work?

Ans = . . .

Study the accurate figure below and then answer questions 91 to 97. All measurements are in centimetres.

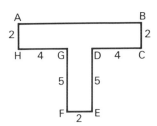

91.   Name a line parallel to AH.   *Ans* = . . .

92.   Name a vertical line.   *Ans* = . . .

93.   Name a horizontal line.   *Ans* = . . .

94.   How many right angles are in this figure?   *Ans* = . . .

95.   How long is AB?   *Ans* = . . . cm

96.   What is the perimeter of this figure?   *Ans* = . . . cm

97.   What is the area of this figure?   *Ans* = . . . cm²

98.   ¾ of the money that I have is $36.00. How much money do I have?   *Ans* = $. . .

99. The cost of a notebook is $1.85 and the cost of a pen is twice as much as a notebook. What is the total cost of two similar pens and a similar notebook?   *Ans* = $...

100. Auntie Pam bought a television set on hire-purchase. She had to make a down payment of $100.00 and then pay $65.00 every month for 12 months. What was the total hire-purchase cost of the television set?   *Ans* = $...

Test **Two**

1. Add   540
         + 36
_____

_____

2. Subtract   876
            − 270
_____

_____

3. Multiply   243
          × 2
_____

_____

4. Divide $6\overline{)426}$

5. $463 - 176 = \ldots$

6. What is the difference between 75 and 25?   *Ans* $= \ldots$

7. What number is 15 less than 105?   *Ans* $= \ldots$

8. When 136 is divided by 7, what is the quotient?

                                             Ans $= \ldots$

9. The sum of three consecutive numbers is 51. Which of these is the largest?   *Ans* $= \ldots$

10. When 3 times a certain number is added to 6, the answer is 30. What is the certain number?   *Ans* $= \ldots$

Complete the following correctly:

11. $326 = \ldots$ tens + 6 ones

12. $218 = 2$ hundreds $+ \ldots$ ones

13. Write in figures: sixty thousand and three   *Ans* $= \ldots$

14. Multiply

    768
   × 70
_____

_____

15. Multiply

    376
   × 63
_____

_____

16. Divide

9338 ÷ 23

Ans = . . .

17. Subtract

h	min
26	20
− 6	35

18. Add

m	cm
6	76
8	48
+	37

19. Divide

$63.45 ÷ 9

Ans = $. . .

20. The difference of two numbers is 58. If the smaller number is 87, what is the bigger number? *Ans* = . . .

Use two signs from here (+, −, ×, ÷), one in each space, to make each statement correct.

21. 6 . . . 4 = 16 . . . 6

22. 8 . . . 5 = 12 . . . 4

23. 16 . . . 8 = 7 . . . 5

24. 14 . . . 14 = 9 . . . 0

25. 5 . . . 3 . . . 1 = 7

26. 12 . . . 4 . . . 2 = 5

27. 6 . . . 3 . . . 2 = 9

28. (3 . . . 5) . . . 3 = 24

Write the answer for each of the following:

29. 5 + 3 × 2 − 4 = . . .

30. 8 × (7 − 3) = . . .

31. (6 − 1) × (5 + 3) = . . .

32. 15 − 4 × 2 + 7 = . . .

33. 4.7 + 12.6 + 0.85 = . . .

34. 16 − 0.96 = . . .

35. 0.27 × 0.06 = . . .

36. 4.09 × 0.08 = . . .

37. 0.612 ÷ 9 = . . .

38. 4.2 ÷ 0.5 = . . .

From the set of numbers {21, 22, 23, 24, 25, 26, 27, 28, 29} pick out the following:

39. The smallest prime number. *Ans* = . . .

40.   The largest prime number.   *Ans* = . . .

41.   The number which is a multiple of 8.   *Ans* = . . .

42.   The largest odd number.   *Ans* = . . .

43.   The smallest even number.   *Ans* = . . .

44.   Through how many degrees does the hour hand of a clock rotate from 2 o'clock to 5 o'clock?   *Ans* = . . . degrees

Study the two figures below.

45.   What is the value of *b*?   *Ans* = . . . degrees

46.   What is the value of *a*?   *Ans* = . . . degrees

47.   What is the value of 2*a*?   *Ans* = . . . degrees

48.   A dealer bought a television set for $800.00 and sold it at a profit of 20%. How much did he sell it for?   *Ans* = $ . . .

49.   A video set which usually costs $1800.00 was reduced by 10%. How much would a customer have to pay for it?
Ans = $ . . .

50.   The sum of the ages of my class teacher, my *twin* sister and me are 44 years. If my class teacher is twice as old as I, how old is she?   *Ans* = . . . years old

51.   Aunt Jane bought a box of candies. She gave $\frac{2}{3}$ of them to her niece and $\frac{1}{4}$ to a friend. What fraction had she left?
Ans = . . .

52.   Twenty pupils from our class watch *Falcon Crest* on TV. If these represent $\frac{2}{3}$ of the class, how many pupils are in the class?   *Ans* = . . . pupils

Each figure below is an isosceles trapezium.

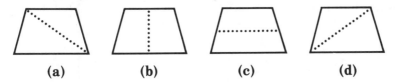

| (a) | (b) | (c) | (d) |

53. In which figure is the broken line a line of symmetry?

$$Ans = \ldots$$

If $a = 3$, $b = 2$, $c = 1$, and $d = 0$, what is the value of:

54. $a + 3b = \ldots$ **56.** $cd + ab = \ldots$

55. $a^2 - c^2 = \ldots$ **57.** $2ab^3 = \ldots$

The total mass of a yam and a potato is 800 g. If the yam is 40 g heavier than the potato:

58. The yam is . . . g **59.** The potato is . . . g

60. If 4 similar ballpoint pens cost \$6.00, what would 10 of these pens cost at the same price? $Ans = \$ \ldots$

61. The bypass bus left Oistin town at 11:45 hours and reached Speightstown at 13:05 hours. How long did the journey take? $Ans = \ldots h \ldots min$

62. An express minibus carries 25 passengers on every trip. How much money is collected after 10 trips if each passenger pays 70¢ for each trip? $Ans = \$ \ldots$

63. Mr Taitt buys 2 L of milk every day. How much must he pay for milk at the end of 1 week (7 days) if 1 L of milk costs \$1.60? $Ans = \$ \ldots$

64. The average of 5 numbers is 45. If 4 of the numbers are 71, 16, 9 and 87, what is the fifth number? $Ans = \ldots$

65. The area of a square is 100 cm^2. What is its perimeter?

$$Ans = \ldots cm$$

The perimeter of the figure on the right is 37 cm.

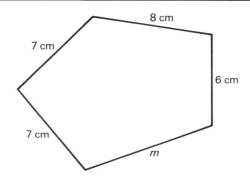

66. What is the length of the side marked m? *Ans* = ... cm

In the diagram to the right the coordinates of P are (4, 2).

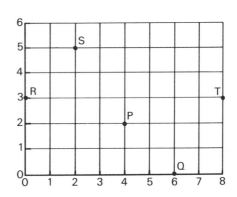

67. The coordinates of Q = (...)
68. The coordinates of R = (...)
69. The coordinates of S = (...)
70. The coordinates of T = (...)
71. What is 10% of $25.40? *Ans* = $...
72. Last Christmas my mother bought a set of glasses for $12.75 and a Pyrex dish for twice as much. How much money in all did she spend on the dish and glasses?

Ans = $...

Complete correctly:

73. 2.4 kg = ...g
74. 5000 g = ...kg

75. A box when half full of sugar weighs 12 kg. What is its weight when it is three quarters full? *Ans* = ...kg

Choose names from here to identify the shapes below (circle, cone, rectangle, parallelogram, cylinder, triangle, cuboid, sphere).

76.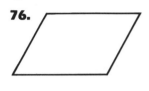

. . .

79.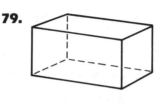

. . .

77.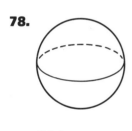

. . .

80.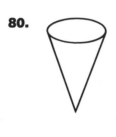

. . .

78.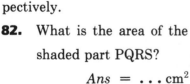

. . .

81.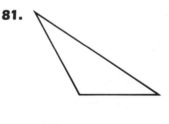

. . .

In the figure to the right ABCD is a square of side 12 cm. P, Q, R and S are the mid points of AB, BC, CD, and AD respectively.

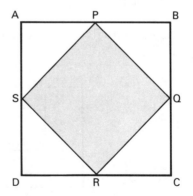

82. What is the area of the shaded part PQRS?

$$Ans = \ldots \mathrm{cm}^2$$

83. How much US currency can be exchanged for BB $102.50 if US $1 = BB $2.05? $Ans = $ US $ \ldots$

Cost price of article   = $120.00

Selling price of article = $90.00

Complete correctly:

84. Loss   *Ans* = $ . . .

85. Loss %   *Ans* = . . . %

The diagram below shows the plan of the floor of the living-room of a house drawn to a scale of 1 cm = 5 m.

86. What is the width of the room in m?   *Ans* = . . . m

87. If the length of the room is 20 m, how many centimetres must represent this on the plan?   *Ans* = . . . cm

88. Deon was born on 15th April, 1976. How old was he on 15th July, 1985?   *Ans* = . . . years . . . months

An aircraft travelled 1050 km in 3 h.

89. What was its speed in km per hour?

Ans = . . . km per hour

90. How long did it take to travel 525 km?   *Ans* = . . . h

Study the accurate figure below and then answer questions 91 to 98.

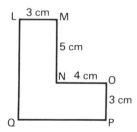

91. Name a line parallel to OP.   *Ans* = . . .

92. Name a horizontal line.   *Ans* = . . .

93. Name a vertical line. $Ans = \ldots$

94. How many right angles are in this figure? $Ans = \ldots$

95. How long is LQ? $Ans = \ldots$ cm

96. How long is QP? $Ans = \ldots$ cm

97. What is the perimeter of this shape? $Ans = \ldots$ cm

98. What is the area of this shape? $Ans = \ldots$ cm^2

In a basketball match Ryan scored 4 times as many goals as his brother Kevin. Together they scored 80 goals.

99. Kevin scored . . . goals.

100. Ryan scored . . . goals.